Connecting to the Internet

A Buyer's Guide

Connecting to the Internet

A Buyer's Guide

Susan Estrada

O'Reilly & Associates, Inc.
103 Morris Street, Suite A
Sebastopol, CA 95472

Connecting to the Internet

by Susan Estrada

Editor: Dale Dougherty

Printing History:

> August 1993:   First Edition.

This book is printed on acid-free paper with 50% recycled content, 10-15% post-consumer waste. O'Reilly & Associates is committed to using paper with the highest recycled content available consistent with high quality.

ISBN: 1-56592-061-9

Table of Contents

List of Figures

List of Tables

Acknowledgments

This is the impossible book made possible and many people deserve thanks for their efforts. First, my husband, Don, and my kids, Chris and Megan, put up with my 18 hour days and gave me hugs when I needed them the most.

The reviewers deserve special thanks, too, for their quick and insightful comments. Dale Dougherty, Tim O'Reilly, Laura Fillmore, Tracy LaQuey Parker, Bruce Cotsonas, Thomas Powell, and Justine Correa were amazing!

Then, there were the folks who pointed me in the right direction on my quest for additional information: Herman Estrada, Jimmy Lang, Pushpendra Mohta, Heather Hughes, Rozeanne Steckler, Mike Bailey, Kathi Stone, Bill Hulley, Firefighter Blaylock, David Wasley, Tony Hain, Tom LaFleur, Barry Gerber, Paul Hoffman, John Curran, Priscilla Houston, Don Mitchell, Diana Whiteside, Joe Simone, Jack Saunders, and Vint Cerf. Special thanks to all of the providers in Dlist for being so prompt about submitting their information and Peter Kaminski who graciously allowed me to reprint his list PDIAL.

My equipment suppliers were invaluable! Thanks to Julie Van Fleet and Gene and Ginny Hallner. Thanks, too, to Lucy Galindo, for being there when I needed her most.

And, finally, thanks to Mike Sierra, Chris Reilley, Donna Woonteiler, Clairemarie Fisher O'Leary, Stephen Spainhour, and Ellie Cutler of O'Reilly, and the staff of Editorial, Inc. who did a nine month job in three weeks.

Introduction

These days, you can't pick up the newspaper or turn on CNN without hearing about the emerging information highways, or the National Information Infrastructure (NII). Everyone is talking about online information and services. The Regional Bell Operating Companies (RBOCs) and the cable industry want to play in the digital sandbox. International giants, as well as smaller companies, are aggressively pursuing on-demand entertainment. The services they want to provide are neither available yet, nor quite defined. We're seeing a merger of three separate industries: telecommunications, broadcasting, and computing, and it's going to take some time before we know what the result will be. Everyone has his or her own opinion about what the electronic future holds and everyone wants to make money from it.

Then there's the Internet. Although primarily a text-based computer network, video and audio applications are starting to be used, both in experimental projects and in production environments. Whether you're just talking about it or already connected to it, the Internet is here—it's working and being used by as many as 15 million people in over 60 countries. The Internet is like a highway, feeding small communities and large cities, and connecting their loops, backroads, and alleyways. The Internet is a viable network solution for information searching and retrieval, access to remote resources, and a powerful communication tool for collaboration with colleagues and customers.

Because of its research origins, some well-publicized government funding, and acceptable use policies that limit commercial use, the Internet has been overlooked or underestimated by many businesses.

Nonetheless, commercial access and use is commonplace, and will very soon (if it doesn't already) make up the largest percentage of traffic on the Internet. This information highway stuff is already happening. If you don't know about it, if you don't get connected, you're going to miss the boat.

The problem is, getting on the boat is not always an easy task. No amount of laudatory trade press can hide the fact that the Internet is not easy to "join." Despite the sudden appearance of introductory books and menuized, graphical applications, the Internet is still considered by many to be a dark mystical underworld where only computer wizards dare to tread.

Perhaps this is because of the confusing terms, the bewildering number of right and wrong solutions, and the incredible choice in service offerings. The term "Internet connection," for example, can mean any number of things, depending on where you are, what you're doing, and what time of the day it is. However, connecting to the Internet isn't rocket science: there's just a lot of background information you've got to know in order to make the physical connection, as well as understanding why you need it and how you're going to use it.

Some people revel in this complexity: memorize about 10,000 acronyms, make sense of a seven layer networking model, crawl around in a closet, become intimate with a bazillion cables and wires, and make sure the gender is bendered correctly. The only way you're going to know how to do this without a lot of wailing, gnashing of teeth, and reading opaque technical manuals is to have done it for ten years as part of your job. Or, you can hire someone.

Fortunately for you, in this era of the "service industry," there are entrepreneurs trying to make money by figuring out and giving the public what it wants, there are idealists trying to change the world, there are benevolent organizations, and there are the big guys (Long Distance Providers and RBOCs) who are stirring into action. All of the above form an ever-expanding group of Internet Providers. They will help you get connected to the Internet. And they will all offer more choices and options than the soft drink industry.

Sounds great, but keep in mind that it's still an infant industry. The rules sometimes change daily. Some service offerings may be experimental and some haven't got all the kinks worked out. The Internet provider industry needs standards for services; it needs definitive solutions. It's also a two-way street: those of us desiring Internet connections need to understand what it is *we* want to do and communicate that effectively to the service providers. Once all the pieces fall into place, life will become easier for everyone. Until then, it might sometimes seem like the electronic version of the Keystone Kops. Just hang on for the ride. It's worth it!

Leading the charge in helping us understand the playing field is Susan Estrada. Her book, *Connecting to the Internet*, defines what the standards should be. It explains the first step in figuring out what it is you want and need with an Internet connection. It is a buyer's guide for Internet connections, telling you what to look for from a provider, what questions you should ask, what your options are, and what the tradeoffs are. After reading this book, you will have a much better idea what type of connection you need, what's involved in securing your own personal connection into Cyberspace, and who can best help you get there for a price you can afford. *Connecting to the Internet* is a brave attempt to bring together all the basics you need in one readable book. This is the guide to jump-starting your connection to the Information Highway.

Tracy LaQuey Parker
Manager, Education Market Development
Cisco Systems, Inc.
Author of *The Internet Companion:*
A Beginner's Guide to Global Networking

1

How the Internet Works

You've heard that millions of people are connected worldwide to a computer network called the Internet. Universities, government agencies, and businesses all use the Internet. Teachers and students use the Internet. Doctors and lawyers use the Internet. You want to use the Internet.

It can be hard to figure out where to start. The Internet is not one place or one company. It is really a descriptive term for a web of thousands of interconnected networks. You wouldn't be far off it you imagined the Internet as a kind of computer amoeba, reaching out and connecting separate islands of computer resources into a seamless web.

Imagine that there were once researchers at a university who learned how useful it was to share their data with each other using a local area network. Now imagine that those researchers wanted to share their data with researchers on a network at another university. The technical problem was how to get two networks to talk to each other. The idea was simple, if not so simple to implement: if you can connect computers on a local area network, why not connect networks in a wide area network? A set of independent physical networks could become a single logical network. In the 70's and 80's, this logical network was created and grew to have global reach; it became known as the Internet.

Interconnecting Networks

On a local area network, the physical link between two computers could be wire, fiber optics or even a "wireless" link using radio frequencies.

These links are usually designed specifically for carrying computer data. On the Internet, the physical link connecting two networks is usually a direct or *dedicated phone line* (sometimes called a *leased line*, as you "lease" it from the phone company). The most common types of dedicated links were originally designed for carrying digitized voice between phone company offices. They work just fine for computer data, but the use of phone lines for computer data means the world of telecommunications and computer networking are intertwined. A dedicated line can be expensive, as it requires the phone company to install and dedicate equipment to your link where it passes through their office. In contrast, a *dialup phone line* has a connection into a phone company office, and can go anywhere from there. These are cheap, as they don't require any special equipment or commitment on the phone company's behalf.

A dialup line is "switched." That is, when you make a long-distance phone call, the phone company may route your call through St. Louis one time and Des Moines the next. The phone company's computers switch traffic to use the best route, depending on the load. A direct line is not switched; it is a route that is reserved for your full-time use. You never have to dial up to "place a call."

You can use a dialup phone line to connect to the Internet with a modem. A modem on one end of the connection converts a stream of bits into a sound wave and a modem on the other end converts the analog signal it receives back into a digital stream. It is possible that data will go through several digital-to-analog and analog-to-digital conversions. Analog lines transmit data at much lower speeds than digital lines because they are limited to the frequencies used for voice transmission, putting an upper limit on the top data rate. Digital services do not have this restriction and are designed for transmitting digital information.

If you think of the Internet as a highway system, a network connection is a road that can handle a certain volume of traffic at a certain speed. There are high-speed network connections, which, like an expressway, can handle a great volume of traffic; the data traveling on that link will get from one place to another very quickly. There are low-speed connections, which are about the same as residential streets, where travel occurs at slower speeds and the volume is light. Any link on the Internet can experience congestion when there's too much traffic and not enough capacity to handle it.

On the Internet, each local network maintains a direct connection to at least one other network, and that network maintains connections to others. In that way, the various networks are interconnected, even though not all of them are directly connected.

The Internet also has some high speed data highways called *backbones*. These are major access points to which lots of networks connect. They are the equivalent of Interstate highways. *ARPAnet*, created in 1969, was the original backbone of the Internet. Today, there's the National Science Foundation (*NSFNET*) backbone, which, like ARPAnet, is funded by the Federal government. Government funding of the Internet supported its use for researchers and educators but it also restricted its use for commercial purposes. These restrictions were known collectively as the Acceptable Use Policy (AUP). In recent years, many restrictions have been relaxed, and the government's role as the financial backer of the Internet has diminished.

One of the most significant changes to the Internet came when a number of access providers formed an alliance known as the Commercial Internet Exchange (*CIX*). CIX established a commercial backbone, separate from NSFNET, that could be used for commericial traffic without restriction. Commercial use of the Internet is now widespread and is clearly driving the growth of the Internet. Internet service providers have a central role in fostering and accommodating this growth. They are the ones connecting more and more people to the Internet for almost any intended use.

It may be hard to keep from confusing what Internet service providers do and what phone companies do. The phone companies supply the dedicated phone lines that Internet service providers use to connect the networks. These phone lines are used for Internet traffic and the Internet service providers install and maintain the switching equipment that directs traffic on the network. If you bring a dedicated line into your business, you are basically paying the phone company for the line and paying the Internet service provider to install and maintain equipment that manages the line at your end and at the provider's end.

A Packet-switched Network

On a local area network, data is sent over the wire in *packets* from one computer to the other. You can think of a packet as an envelope containing data. Like an envelope sent through the post office, each packet contains the address of its destination on the network. As packets travel on the network, each computer examines the address of the packet to see if it should pick it up.

The Internet is a packet-switched network. Just like local area networks, packets are sent out over the link to the Internet. An important piece of equipment called a *router* sits on the local network and looks at packets. It picks those that do not have a local address and "routes" them to other networks, as shown in Figure 1.1. You can think of the router as functioning like a local post office that recognizes local mail and knows how to route mail to other post offices to reach remote destinations.

In all likelihood, a packet that gets out on the Internet will go through several networks to reach its destination. Remember, the networks are interconnected, not directly connected to one another. In the same way, a letter given to the local post office might be routed to a larger regional hub and from there to another local post office nearest the destination. Routers determine the path that data travels on the Internet, switching packets from one network to another. The speed of a transmission is very much dependent on the path that the data travels and the amount of traffic on each of the networks that it passes through.

Any message that you send on the Internet is broken up into one or more packets, and those packets can travel independently, possibly taking different paths to the same destination. If one link is down, the packets can be re-routed over other links. Once the packets reach the destination, they are reassembled.

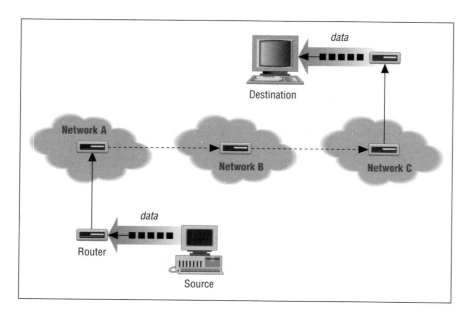

Figure 1-1. Routers direct traffic between networks

A Communications Protocol

The unifying principle of the Internet is a suite of communications protocols called *TCP/IP* (Transmission Control Protocol/Internet Protocol). A communications protocol allows different kinds of computers using different operating systems to communicate with each other. TCP/IP specifies an addressing scheme for computers on the Internet, how to route data from one network to another, and how to deliver the data to a process or program running on a computer.

The addressing scheme is known as *IP addressing*. An IP address is a number (e.g., 128.66.12.4) that identifies the network and a specific host computer on that network. The IP address can be mapped (or translated) into a host computer's domain name. "ora.com" is the network domain at O'Reilly & Associates; it can be further subdivided into east and west subdomains or subnets, that refer to different local area networks at O'Reilly. Each computer in that domain has its own name: stone, pebble, rock, etc. Therefore, the domain name of a specific computer in the West Coast O'Reilly office might be: stone.west.ora.com.

In the United States, there are different classifications of domains. The major domains are "com" for commercial, as in "ora.com"; "edu" for educational, as in "berkeley.edu"; "gov" for government, as in "house.gov"; "net" for network providers, as in "uu.net"; and "org" for non-profit companies, such as "usenix.org". Another domain naming convention uses two-letter country codes to specify top-level domains. Some examples are: "au" for Australia, "ca" for Canada, "it" for Italy, and "us" for United States. For instance, the domain name of the WELL (Whole Earth 'Lectronic Link) located across the bay from San Francisco, California is: well.sf.ca.us.

Each packet of data has a header (similar to the "From" and "To" information on an envelope) with an IP address that specifies its destination. IP addressing allows systems on the network, which run IP software, to make routing decisions. For instance, they can determine whether the address is a destination on a local area network or on a remote network. Each system on the network maintains a routing table that identifies the appropriate route to a remote network. The routing table does not point directly to the destination, but to a gateway called the "next hop." Thus, data travels from one hop to the next along a path that finally reaches its destination on another network.

Once data reaches its destination, it must be delivered to an application that is waiting for it. The data arrives in a single stream and the packets must be distributed to the appropriate applications. A unique port number included in the packet's header information identifies the correct application. It is not really too important for our purposes to understand how this is done, only that TCP/IP takes care of it in a very general way. To learn more about TCP/IP, there are several excellent books listed in the bibliography. For the most part, we are concerned with the applications themselves and how much traffic they generate, not the underlying protocols that allow them to work over a network. TCP/IP allows Internet applications like File Transfer Protocol (*FTP*), TELNET, electronic mail, Usenet News and Gopher to run on the Internet.

Internet Connections

Generally speaking, you don't pay for what you do on the Internet, you pay for your connection. (This practice may be changing, and some network providers may begin to meter usage; even so, your usage will be indexed by the type of connection you have.) That's why it's important to understand how the Internet works. The price of an Internet connection is based on the capacity of the link—its ability to carry traffic at a certain speed. The larger the capacity, the more it will cost but the more traffic it will carry.

Understanding how you want to use the Internet will help you determine how much traffic you will generate, and also how fast that traffic needs to move on the network. On the one hand, you don't want to pay for capacity that you don't need and won't use. On the other, you want ample capacity or you'll find that you've created a traffic jam and the network is less productive. It is important to plan for the future. Most headaches are caused by not anticipating the popularity of the network among all users in an organization and predicting the growth in traffic as those users find more applications for the Internet connectivity.

In the next chapter, I explain in more detail how speed is measured on the Internet and examine network performance as a whole.

2

Understanding Network Performance

When it comes to data communications, speed rules. Faster links enable more interesting applications to move more data and provide for more users. Having a larger connection to the Internet will allow you to complete tasks more quickly and increase your efficiency. Speed isn't everything, but it is a useful guide to understanding and evaluating network performance.

This chapter explains speed and its relationship to network performance. You'll also get the big picture of how the Internet is linked together, and how different providers interact to determine the actual quality of connection.

Understanding Speed and Size

The first thing to understand is the speed and size of your connection to the Internet. If you have done a proper evaluation of your needs, you will have a good idea if you require a low, medium, or high speed link. The following sections will help you understand what you can do at each level and will reinforce your decision to choose a particular type of connection.

Measuring Speed and Size

The speed of a network connection is usually stated in *bits-per-second* (bps). That is, speed is measured by the number of 1s and 0s that can be transmitted over the wire in a single second. These speeds are measured in kilobits, megabits, or gigabits:

```
kilobits (kpbs)=Thousand bits-per-second
megabits (mbps)=Million bits-per-second
gigabits (gbps)=Trillion bits-per-second
```

The size of a set of data, or data file, is usually expressed in *bytes*, or segments of eight bits. One byte can be used to represent a single character. The size of data files is measured in kilobytes, megabytes, or gigabytes:

```
kilobytes (KB) =Thousand bytes
megabytes (MB) =Million bytes
gigabytes (GB) =Trillion bytes
```

Data files, at the time of transfer, are of fixed, known sizes. They can be compared to the amount of water that would fit into a container. There are various container sizes from one cup of water to a swimming pool full of water.

When moving a data file across the network, the time it takes for the files to be transferred can be compared to a hose that transports water. Depending on the size of hose used, different amounts of water can be transported in a fixed period of time. Imagine the difference in the amount of water delivered in one minute by a garden hose and a 2.5-inch fire hose. A garden hose delivers 10 gallons-per-minute while a fire hose delivers 250 gallons-per-minute. If you're going to fill your swimming pool, the fire hose would fill it much more quickly than the garden hose.

No Dry Pipes

In 1992, California experienced a severe drought and mandatory water restrictions were put into place. There was plenty of water available in the Colorado River, the source of water for California. The population of Southern California is growing at a rate such that demand exceeds the capacity of the system. During the drought, local reservoirs were not available to meet the additional demand. More water could have been transported to Southern California but the system did not have enough capacity in the existing transport pipes to move additional water. That's a good reminder about building extra capacity into any system, whether the pipes are carrying water or data.

Using Pipes to Transfer Data

Large pipes bring water from reservoirs to local water companies; smaller pipes bring water from wells to your house; and even smaller pipes make water available in your home. Different sizes of pipes are used depending on the volume of water that is transported from one site to another. The transport of data on a network can be viewed in the same way.

Just like a garden hose handles less water than a fire hose, data communication pipes, sometimes referred to as links, handle different amounts of data per second. The amount of data a pipe can handle is referred to as its bandwidth.

Figure 2-1 compares data pipe capacities to equivalent water pipe capacities. This analogy will give you a sense of the magnitude of the differences between the different size of data pipes.

You can see that with a 2400 bits-per-second connection, the equivalent of a cup-per-second could be moved. At 14.4 kilobits-per-second, a popular speed for modems, the equivalent of a quart-per-second could be moved. At 45 mbps, the equivalent of three hottubs-per-second could be moved.

Comparing Transfer Speeds

Different amounts of data are different sizes. You can get a sense of perspective about the size of data files if you compare them to more familiar quantities shown in Figure2-2.

For example, it would be easy to transfer a two-page e-mail message. Its equivalent measure is 7 cups of data, so even at 2400 bits-per-second (1 cup-per-second), it will only take 7 seconds to transfer. On the other hand, when transferring the *Wizard of Oz* (50 gallons of data), you'd have to wait 13 minutes for the entire transfer at 2400 bits-per-second.

The Steady Stream

Real-time applications, live video or audio for example, are more like streams or rivers of data than containers of data. The data is not a single file that you can go pick up. It is generated as a stream of data and must be transported instantaneously for it to be seen or heard without interruption. A pipe big enough to transport the whole stream all at once is needed.

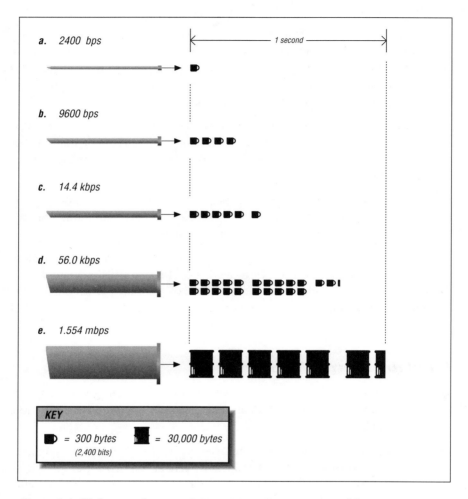

Figure 2-1. Higher speed connections move a greater amount of data

Because most audio and video on the Internet is still experimental, there are no firm statistics on the size of "flows." Video and audio data flows depend on a host of different parameters (the resolutions of the images, how many sites are communicating simultaneously, and more). These parameters have an impact on how much data can be sent or received on a video or audio Internet connection.

An Internet audio stream is as much as 64 kbps per live session. In the wonderful world of water, this data stream would be equivalent to 1.7 gallons per second: about 10 garden hoses going full blast. Internet video

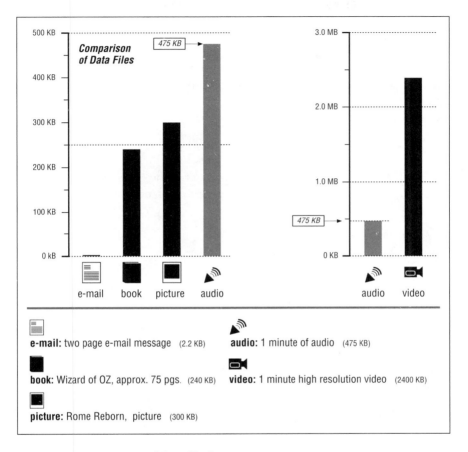

Figure 2-2. Comparison of data files by size

streams are about 128 kbps per live session. This is equivalent to approximately 3.3 gallons-per-second. This stream is compared to 19 garden hoses going full blast or one fire hose. A different kind of comparison of data file sizes is shown in Figure 2-2.

Internet Connection Speeds

Internet connection speeds come in slow, fast, and faster configurations. Slower speeds are usual with dialup Internet connections as well as inexpensive dedicated connections. Faster speeds are usually limited to dedicated line connections.

Slow, but Sure

The slowest speeds used on the Internet generally match the speeds available with modems. Common speeds today are 2400, 9600, and 14,400 kbps. You can get higher speeds of up to 57,600 bits-per-second with compression. Compression is a technique that reduces the files by squishing them into a smaller space. V.42bis is a common compression standard and compresses at up to a 4:1 ratio. This means your file could take 1/4 of the time to be transferred compared to the same file uncompressed.

Table 2-1 shows common modem speeds and the standards they use. In addition, modems may support compression standards, such as LAPM and MNP5 (V.42bis).

Table 2-1. Modem Speeds and Standards

Bit-per-second	Standard
1200 bps	V.22
2400 bps	V.22bis
9.6 kbps	V.32, V.3
14.4 kbps	V.32bis

The modems at both ends of any telephone link have to use the same standards in order for the standards to work. If you buy a fast modem with compression standards, be sure that your network service provider's modems use the same standards; otherwise, you won't use the top speed of your modem. There is a new standard for modems under development called V.Fast. It is not widely available at this time but is expected to be so in the next year or two. There are also proprietary modem protocols that can achieve even faster speeds, but both ends of the link must have modems from the same manufacturer to realize the top speed.

At modem speeds, much of the functionality of the Internet is possible. Figure 2-3 takes data files and shows the ideal time it would take to move them at different speeds. Of course, we do not live in an ideal world, even on the Internet, so expect these times to fluctuate. However, the speeds shown will help you establish realistic expectations for throughput at various speeds.

14.4 (14,400) kbps is six times faster than 2400 bits-per-second. This means that the time needed to transfer many large files (QuickTime videos for example) could be reduced from an hour to ten minutes. However, at the speeds listed in Figure2-3, it is still impractical to

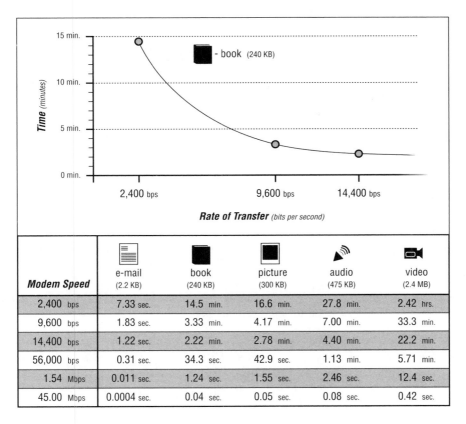

Figure 2-3. Chart of ideal speed versus function

transfer larger files on the network. For example, if you collect an Internet Talk Radio file, you will wait over two hours at 14.4 kbps. However, everything is relative. One user regularly transfers 5-10 mega-byte files over the Internet at 14.4 kbps because it is quick, inexpensive, and reliable. His other choice was overnight mail delivery. The Internet won.

Even if you are willing to wait, steady stream applications (such as video) cannot be used at these speeds. As better compression algorithms are invented and applied to the video and audio streams, it may become real-istic to have a video and audio connection at the higher modem speeds.

Modem links will be most useful for those with low and medium impact applications. Generally, individuals and small businesses will find these affordable and adequate for their needs, at least in the short term.

From 20 to 2 for $288

I began writing this book from home using a 2400 bits-per-second modem. I was transferring drafts to my editor over the Internet. Each chapter took approximately 20 minutes to transfer. Before long I read my own writing and came to my senses. I purchased a V.32bis modem with V.42bis compression for $288. After half a day of configuration frustration, I was able to transfer the same size chapters in less than two minutes.

Bigger Is Better

Higher speed links normally mean dedicated telephone line connections using digital links. The modem links discussed above are run on analog lines. The capacity of analog lines is limited. Using dedicated lines and speeds of 56 kbps or better, you can begin to take full advantage of the Internet's wealth of resources.   Within the telecommunications industry, the speed of 1.544 mbps is known as " T1" or "DS1" for "Digital Signal Level 1.") 45 mpbs is known as "T3" or "DS3."

ISDN, Integrated Services Digital Network, is a kind of dial up access over a digital link. It can support speeds of up to 128 kbps. ISDN is discussed in more detail in Chapter4, *Choosing Your Network Provider.*

Table 2-2 shows the sample files and the time it takes to transfer data at the speeds of 56 kbps, 1.544 mbps, and 45 mbps. These numbers are based on the type of links readily available from most telephone companies. There are other speeds available as well.

Table 2-2. Roundtrip times for Local Connections measured in milliseconds. These are for digital lines.

Speed	Time
9.6 kbps	200 ms
19.2 kbps	45 ms
56 kbps	9 ms
1.544 mbps	7 ms
10 mbps	5 ms

At 56 kbps, your video capabilities are limited. Above that, at 1.544 mbps and 45 mbps, most applications are easy to accomplish on the Internet. In seconds, files can be transferred. Steady stream data can be transmitted readily, although caution must be taken to avoid swamping the link. That is, you might be able to transmit video over the connection just fine, but users doing other things will notice the impact. At 1.544 mbps, 12 streams of data will completely fill your link. At 45 mbps, 355 steady streams of data will fill your link.

Typically, 56 kbps connections are used by medium-sized businesses. Small businesses with high impact needs may find these speeds reasonable, too. They are generally too expensive for individuals. Larger businesses will use T1 (1.544 mbps) connections. For those sites that don't need or can't afford T1 access, they can sometimes get a "sub-rate" or "fractional" T1 that uses only a "fraction" of the individual channels (called "DSOs" in telco-speak) available on a T1. (Some vendors call this "T1 low-volume.") When you start to need more capacity, more channels can be made available to you. Just think of it as buying a huge water pipe from the utility company and asking them to open the valve a little bit more as you use more water. In most cases, the vendor is forced to sell a minimum number of channels (for example, 4 for a speed of 256k) by the local phone company, so your options may be limited. Also keep in mind that there will be some break-even point where it's more effective to go with the full T1. For example, you probably should get the full T1 if you need more than 12 channels. Ask your vendor to supply quotes for the full range of speeds that they offer. 45 mbps connections are used by sites with very high impact applications such as supercomputer centers or research universities.

Gigabits and Gigabytes

There is a lot of discussion about higher speeds for the Internet—on the order of gigabits-per-second. Several research groups across the country are developing these connections and experimenting with applications that can take advantage of the speed. The growth of the Internet—in the number of people using it and the data available on it—means this kind of network will be necessary in the near future.

For the most part, high-speed, gigabit-per-second lines will be used only for network backbone circuits (that's the equivalent of your city's water main). It will be quite a while before individuals and small businesses need that kind of speed.

Dem Bones, MBones, and Backbones

The MBone is the Multicast Backbone of the Internet. The idea is to construct a semi-permanent IP multicast testbed to broadcast technical meetings such as the *IETF* and support continued experimentation between meetings. This is a cooperative, volunteer effort. At this time, there is not a sufficient infrastructure to provide this service on a significant scale, although commercial products are expected to help in a few years.

Internet Talk Radio debuted in March 1993, broadcasting the program "Geek of the Week" over the MBone. Internet Talk Radio will expand to a full featured radio program, not unlike NPR, with news, travel and leisure, food, and events stories. Executive producer and author Carl Malamud views ITR prophetically: "When NBC broadcast its first radio program in the early 1920's, there were only a few people with radio sets. This quickly grew to become a new medium with millions of listeners. The Internet is poised for similar growth."

Backbones

You can think of backbones as the spines of the Internet, connecting the individual and organization links of the Internet together. A network backbone is made up of telephone circuits which connect routers together. Everyone using the network and traveling the same path will share backbone circuits. In most cases, each different network provider will have their own backbone at their choice of speed. Most of the larger networks have backbones of 1.544 mbps or 45 mbps telephone lines. Smaller networks may only have backbones of 14.4 kpbs or 56 kbps. Your connection should not be larger than your provider's backbone speed, because you'll end up with a guaranteed bottleneck.

End-to-end Performance

Because the Internet is a network of networks, data traveling across the Internet may pass through many different provider's backbones on its way to its destination. This means that the speed and quality of connections depend on the path chosen to the destination, as shown in Figure 2-4. If you have a 1.544 mbps connection, but pass through a 56 kbps backbone somewhere, your effective link to points on the other side of that backbone will be only 56 kbps. Additionally, if you pass through a backbone that is congested, your data will be slowed down on its path. The performance of the network is a result of the quality of the path the data travels from end to end.

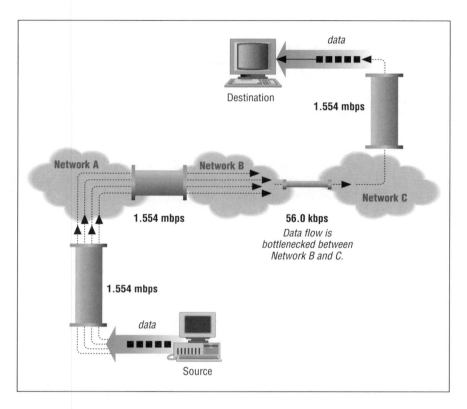

Figure 2-4. Network performance is affected by the speed of each connection along the path that data travels

Some average network performance criteria can be used as baselines for measurements of end-to-end performance of a data path. One criterion is the average roundtrip time of data on a particular path. Measurements for the connection from your site into your provider's backbone are shown in Table 2-2 on Page 14. These figures are averages and may vary slightly. Different types of communications links will result in higher roundtrip times. For example, if frame relay, a special packet link, is used at 56 kbps, the delay is 40 ms instead of 9 ms.

Roundtrip time can also be measured on the total path the data has to travel to reach its destination. In general, if the end-to-end roundtrip time exceeds 500 milliseconds (.5 seconds), noticeable delays will occur in file transfers and data displayed on local computers. You feel like you are typing too fast because you can't see the characters displayed on your screen right away. These delays may be tolerable for some users, but aggravating to others.

Another valuable measurement of end-to-end performance of a particular connection is availability or reliability. This can be measured in many different ways. Proper ways to measure it take into account all of the components in a connection including links, routers, and other equipment necessary to ensure that data can be moved through the network. One provider sends a small amount of data to each of its customer's sites every minute to measure its availability. If the data is lost, the provider knows that the site is no longer available. Using this type of measurement, the average availability of their network over one year was 99.94 percent. This means that their customers, on average, were able to use the network 8754 hours per year out of a total available 8760 hours.

Summary

Your local link speed and the overall network performance will determine the actual functionality of your connection. Most individuals and small businesses will find modem connections adequate. Medium and large businesses need higher speed dedicated line connections to serve their users. Everyone must be aware of overall network performance and its potential effect on their connection to the rest of the Internet.

3

How Will You Use the Internet?

Deciding which type of connection is right for you and where to get it can be confusing. Preparation is key. You will need to examine how you plan to use the Internet. This will help you decide which level of service is best for you.

This chapter profiles different types of Internet users and then poses three basic questions that will help you assess how you plan to use the Internet.

Who Connects to the Internet?

All kinds of individuals and organizations are connected to the Internet. Some individuals connect from home for personal use. Others work from home. Almost every university is connected to the network, and an increasing number of K-12 schools as well. More and more businesses, large and small, are connected to the Internet. It can allow a small business to reach its customers directly, just as it can help large companies improve communications among independent units. A research organization might use the Internet to transmit scientific data for processing to a regional supercomputer site. An increasing number of non-profit groups and governmental agencies are getting on the Internet, as they realize that they have a mission to make information available for as many people as possible.

I will cover connectivity options by profiling the needs of three types of users: individuals, small businesses, and large organizations. See if you can recognize your situation in the descriptions. Your needs may differ, so take them into account during the planning process.

Individual Users

Individual users who obtain their own connection to the Internet may have different motivations for getting connected. They may even be connecting from places other than home, such as someone who travels a lot and connects from a hotel. They may also be individual users in large corporations that do not have a networking infrastructure.

Most individuals use the Internet in the same way, however, primarily sending and receiving electronic mail. Increasingly, individual users are discovering ways to to look for information on the Internet or download files. As user interfaces improve and the cost of higher speed connections goes down, individuals will find themselves making greater use of the resources of the Internet.

There are a few characteristics that typify an individual user. The user's equipment consists of a personal computer and a modem. The computer can be a PC running DOS, or running Windows, a Macintosh, Amiga, or even UNIX-based workstations. These computers have hard disks ranging from 40 to 160 megabytes, adequate for personal needs. The typical modem operates at 2400-bits-per-second, although much faster modems are increasingly affordable. Along with the modem, it is necessary to have communications software, which may be a simple terminal emulation program. Popular communications packages are Microphone, Procomm, Telix, Telemate, Crosstalk, White Knight, Versaterm, and MacIntercomm. These packages allow you to use your modem over a phone line to communicate with a computer at your office, bulletin boards, and information services such as America Online, Delphi, and CompuServe.

Small Businesses

By definition, a small business has perhaps 50 employees, usually at a single site. Not everyone would want or need Internet access; usually a smaller number, five to ten, find it necessary and valuable.

Each person in the company may have a personal computer or there may be only a few available for shared usage. The key consideration is whether the company's computers are connected via a local area network

---

No Room Is Ever Big Enough

The capacity of hard disks has risen as the prices have fallen. It is easy to lose track of how much disk storage you are actually using. Yet running out of room on a disk is still a problem, especially if you are going to be downloading lots of graphics or sound files. I have two children, ages three and five, who managed to use up 40 megabytes of diskspace on my home computer by recording sounds in one of their "kid" programs. When it was time to do my taxes, I had to rearrange the hard disk to make room. It reminded me that disk space is limited and you can use it up quickly.

(LAN). Without a LAN, the company really has a set of individual users fitting the previous profile. Before considering a connection to the Internet, the company should investigate setting up a local area network for its users, and then provide a connection from the LAN to the Internet.

Local area networks are becoming widespread. (I'm even thinking about rewiring my house for one!) Examples of popular ones are Ethernet, token ring, Novell Netware, Banyan Vines, Lan-manager, Lantastic, and Appletalk. Some require special interfaces or additional software to support an Internet connection. Check with your computer store or the manufacturer's literature to see if your LAN supports connectivity to TCP/IP networks.

If the small company has a local area network, users will likely have some experience sharing files with each other and using electronic mail for communication. By adding Internet connectivity, users can share files or exchange e-mail with people outside the company.

A LAN usually has a single computer that acts as a file server for central storage of files; the storage capacity of file servers is usually expandable so that using up disk space is not a primary concern.

Large Organizations

A corporation with several offices, a university or a research lab, and a government agency are examples of large organizations. These organizations may have thousands of employees, not all located in the same building. Just as with a small business, not everyone needs access to the Internet, but the number of potential users might be fairly significant, 500 or so.

Large organizations have complex computing environments, often with one of almost every kind of computer. Larger departmental computers are connected to groups of Macintoshes or PCs. The organization is much more likely to have multiple local area networks, some connected to each other and some not.

There is an MIS department or some group whose responsibility is to administer the systems and provide support for hundreds of users. There is a central electronic mail system to support internal company communications. Security is an important consideration, since there are so many computers to manage. The corporation may have an Internet connection but users may be on a system or LAN that is not allowed direct access for security or other reasons. Because many of the computing resources are centrally managed, getting a direct Internet connection for an individual or a department may involve discussions at the corporate level. There has to be some high-level awareness that the potential benefits of Internet access outweigh the security or productivity concerns.

How To Assess Your Requirements

Developing answers to three questions will help you understand your requirements for a network connection:

- How will you use your Internet connection?

- Who is going to use the connection?

- How much value do you place on getting a connection and what can you afford?

All of these questions are important, but one may be the overriding factor in your decision-making process. The pragmatic view is that cost determines which type of connection you purchase. This is even more true if you are getting a connection for the first time and less true if you already have a sense of the value of the Internet and are upgrading your capacity.

Even if you have a limited budget, don't overlook planning. If you are trying to convince your boss or your spouse of the value of a better grade connection, a needs assessment that takes into account short- and long-term requirements will highlight factors other than just price. Most importantly, planning can prepare you to talk intelligently with access providers and allow you to evaluate their services.

How Will You Use Your Internet Connection?

While there are many possible applications of an Internet connection and internetworking in general, we will survey the range of uses with the following topics:[†]

* Electronic mail
* Public forums or conferences
* Collaborative projects
* Information resources
* Real-time chatting
* Providing information online
* Audio and video conferencing

Electronic Mail

The most widely used facility on the Internet is electronic mail. Generally speaking, e-mail is a low-impact use. That is, e-mail messages aren't very big and don't need to travel at high speeds to be effective. Of greater importance is whether you want to receive e-mail messages immediately as they come in, or have them held for you to be picked up in a single batch. This is a result of whether you stay connected to the Internet all the time or connect at different times throughout the day or night.

On an average, a novice user will receive between 10 and 20 e-mail messages per day. However, more active Internet users can easily get 50

---

† For a more detailed discussion, see*The Whole Internet User's Guide & Catalog,* by Ed Krol (O'Reilly & Associates, 1992).

to 100 messages, and serious users can get 300 messages per day and more. (A two-week vacation becomes a very serious thing at this point— imagine coming home to 3,000 letters in your mailbox!)

A recent development for mail on the Internet is an enhanced form called MIME (Multipurpose Internet Mail Extensions). MIME lets you attach voice messages, video, or pictures to an ordinary e-mail message. This can be a very effective communication tool, but be aware that MIME is a high-impact use, and also requires the equipment to produce the audio and video. As a high-impact use, MIME is only practical to consider for high speed connections.

Just because e-mail is a low-impact use does not mean that it is any less significant in value. The ability to communicate with people worldwide and find others who share a common interest or profession, independent of location, is a wonderous thing. E-mail is a strange hybrid of a type-written letter and a phone conversation. There are a number of people who know each other only through their e-mail exchanges.

It is also worth considering whether you pay for the e-mail messages that you send or receive. CompuServe, MCIMail, and others do charge you per message in addition to connect-time charges. Most Internet access providers do not charge you per message but some may charge you according to the amount of space that the files containing your messages occupy. If you are going to use e-mail heavily, an Internet connection can be a better value than CompuServe and others.

Public Forums or Conferences

You can participate in thousands of different public forums and confer-ences. *USENET* News is the most widely used forum with newsgroups (topics) for nearly every subject or interest. Generally speaking, your participation occurs during interactive sessions, during which you do a lot of reading and a little typing. (The people who are exceptions to this rule, you will discover, can be annoying.) You won't download or upload much data (getting data from somewhere else or putting data somewhere else), so this is considered a low-impact use.

However, if you want an entire USENET newsfeed delivered to your own computers, you must be prepared to handle approximately 45 megabytes of data *per day*. Typical individuals and small business users cannot handle this amount of traffic or its storage requirements. You need approximately 280 megabytes of disk space to store seven days of news.

You don't have to receive a full newsfeed; you can select specific news-groups, cutting down on the traffic and the storage requirement. If handled with care, a select USENET newsfeed can be a low- to medium-impact application.

Large organizations with a diverse user base usually find it more practical to get a large newsfeed that allows users to read the news at their site. This keeps the link free for other applications. A full newsfeed should be considered a medium-impact use.

Many other conferencing systems involve telnetting to someone else's computer and using interactive sessions. These are low-impact uses because there is not much data being transmitted at one time.

Collaborative Projects

A collaborative electronic project involves working as a team with others who are at different locations. Depending on the nature of the data being transported, participation in a collaborative project can be low-, medium-, or high-impact use.

For example, the initial Global Schoolhouse project was a collaboration that spanned three months and involved 60 people throughout the U.S. and the U.K. The primary method of communication during the planning process was e-mail. About 600 messages were exchanged during the month of planning; that's about 30 per day. Since the traffic was relatively low, and the messages contained only text, the impact on any network connection was low.

In contrast, chemists in Minnesota, Ohio, and Washington are working together to develop and maintain a large software package for computa-tional chemistry. As part of a collaborative software development project, they are writing, compiling, testing, and debugging the software code at various locations. The software is kept on one machine while the network is used to shift updates back and forth. File sharing, file transfer, e-mail exchanges, and TELNET access are all important. Because new releases of the software come out every four to six months, data is moved through the network on a regular basis requiring a larger network connec-tion for all participants. This collaboration would be considered a medium- to high-impact use.

When you are looking at your own situation, consider all aspects of a potential collaboration. Think about files that need to be shared. Think about ways you will communicate with your colleagues. Think about how often you need to communicate. Be especially aware of short schedules or quick turnaround times that make new demands of your connection. Think about the number of people working on the collaboration from your site. If there are a number concentrated locally, you need to account for their concurrent use of the network connection.

Normally, individuals and small businesses will find collaboration to be a low- to medium-impact use. Large businesses are likely to find that many such collaborations are in progress, the sum of which may be equivalent to a high-impact use.

Explore Information Resources

If you are planning to use the Internet for accessing its wealth of information, you need to figure out how often you intend to transfer information from or to your local site. You also need to figure out the size of the data. In many cases, you will browse information online with an application like *Gopher* or *WAIS*, and retrieve text files, a low-impact use. However, if you find something you want to begin creating your own archives for use on your computer, you can jump into medium- to high-impact use.

Data files vary in size tremendously depending on the type of data included. Text files are usually the smallest, while anything with graphics or audio is quite large. It is an important to evaluate the size of files since their size will determine the impact of the transfer.

Real-time Chatting

Internet Relay Chat (IRC) and Talk are communications tools that allow you to interact with each other people in real-time. What you type at your keyboard is displayed not only on your screen but on the screen of the person at the other end. Internet Relay Chat and Talk are both low-impact applications. You are only sending as much data as fast as you can type.

Individual users will find these fun. Small businesses and businesses may find these useful or wasteful.

Providing Information Online

Anyone with a network connection can become an information provider. If you have prepared or collected information that is useful to others, you can easily use your Internet connection to distribute it. You might send the information to interested people by e-mail. You might also make it available on your network for others to access. Because you can't always predict how many people will come to get that information, the incoming traffic could be marginal or significant: a number of sites have been shocked by the experience of having thousands of Internet users come to access their database and use up the site's entire connection capacity.

If you are an individual or small business with a limited budget, it might be more cost effective to give your data to someone else who will make it available on the network for you. A number of Internet service providers allow you to put databases online, on their machine, for a fee. Generally, you pay for how much space you occupy on their system. The provider makes sure that people can access your database over a high speed connection and that you can access it yourself to update it as necessary, using a lower cost connection. Companies that provide this service are listed in Appendix A.

Even large businesses may want to consider using a professional database provider as the home for data. This will keep your link free for your own users. And you won't have to bother with setting up, monitoring, and maintaining your own database computer.

Audio and Video Conferencing

Multimedia applications do exist on the Internet but they are data-intensive and require high speed connections. Video conferencing is an example. Shared whiteboards and live audio sessions are other examples. Imagine seeing and talking with your colleagues anywhere on the Internet in an instant. Imagine attending professional conferences by watching a live video transmission from the conference that is sent over the Internet to your workstation.

Most of the video conferencing systems on the Internet are still in the experimental stages. As they mature, they will become easier to install and use. There are many broadcast-type video conferences today. Large businesses can take advantage of video conferencing with a high speed connection. Until the information infrastructure changes significantly, individuals and small businesses will be unable to afford connections suitable for video and audio tranmission in real-time. Multimedia applications may become easier to implement in a year or two.

Figure 3-1. Global schoolhouse demonstrates multimedia network application

Who Will Be Using the Connection?

If you are an individual, the answer to this question is obvious. If you are either a small or a large business, it may not be so obvious. Usually, 10% of the people use 90% of the capacity of your connection. If you adequately predict the needs of the top 10% of your users, you will probably decide on the right size of connection. You do need to make an effort to find the right 10%. Talk to the different groups in your company. If you have experience with high-impact local users, ask them about their planned use for an Internet connection. If you have a group that needs the connection for a special project, find out what they are going to do. Scientists or engineers will have special requirements.

Another item to consider for medium to large businesses is the total number of people actively using the connection. If you have people who are running low-impact applications, but there are 30,000 of those people, demand on your network will be high. My experience leads me to believe that it takes from six to nine months for new users to become comfortable with navigating the Internet. As better user interfaces to the network become available, along with improved training materials and user guides, the learning curve will go down quickly. In general, take into account that usage will ramp up over a period of time.

What Is the Value of a Connection and What Can You Afford?

Justifying the budget for an Internet connection is not simple in these tough economic times. And, contrary to what many believe, the Internet is not free.

When analyzing the value of an Internet connection, it is helpful to have a "measuring stick." For individuals, you can compare the cost of an Internet connection to the cost of using the telephone. Say the cost of a telephone varies but is about $10 per month. You pay extra for long distance charges based on the amount of time you are talking. Look at your monthly telephone bill: do you think the Internet will be as useful as your phone? Are you willing to spend the same amount of money? Remember, you may find e-mail is cheaper than phone to communicate long distance with a number of people.

An Internet connection can make it possible to reduce the amount of time or effort required to perform certain tasks. If you can get information on the Internet that you'd have to get otherwise by driving to the library, how much have you saved? Look at the cost savings and the good will generated from providing sales and customer support online. Evaluate the potential of collaborative partnerships established over the Internet. Find out how much you might save in messenger and overnight delivery fees if you use e-mail or file transfer programs to deliver time-sensitive documents.

There are also things you can do on the Internet that are not practical to do by postal mail, by phone, in print, or any other means. How often do you have the opportunity to address 3000 people in a public forum and state your opinion? How important is it for you to follow the latest developments on an important subject, and be able to respond immediately?

Businesses spend much more money than individuals on their phone. They usually have sophisticated phone systems that are seen as part of the company's basic infrastructure, as essential as desks and chairs. Is your Internet connection going to be as useful as a phone system to your business? It could be, and perhaps everyone in the company should have access. It might allow your business to expand in new ways.

One provider's estimated cost of an Internet connection for a site of 15,000 users was about 8 cents per month per user. The same connection for 100 users would cost about $12.50 per month. When compared to a minimum cost of $15 per month for a phone, the Internet seems like a bargain. In most cases, the cost of an Internet connection will be far less than an equivalent telephone connection and far more valuable in the long run. An average individual user spends $20 to $30 monthly on an Internet connection which compares favorably with the cost of a telephone line.

Questions for Evaluation

You should review these questions and use them to determine whether your usage will result in a low, medium, or high impact on the network connection. When you complete the list, you will have defined your needs for discussion with Internet providers:

- How many people will be reading mail? How much mail will they get?
- Will MIME be useful to my staff within the next year or two?
- Do I have the equipment or software to support MIME, or will I be getting it in the next year or two? (Computer with a microphone, video camera)
- Do I want a USENET newsfeed? How much data?
- Do I have any other conferencing applications that I know about that will cause me to move lots of data back and forth?
- Will I or my site be participating in any collaborations? If yes, how many will there be and how large will they be?
- Does my office have separate locations, branch offices (include home offices)?
- Would my work benefit from collaborating with others electronically, and retrieving documents relevant to my work?
- Will I or my site be doing any large downloads or uploads of data? Will they be on a regular schedule? Will they be often or occasional?
- Do I have data that I want others to access via the Internet? How much data do I have? Where do I want to store the data? Is it less expensive to have someone else store the data online?
- Am I concerned about security issues?
- Is there anyone at my site who will need video conferencing?
- Is there anyone at my site who will need audio conferencing?

- Do I have workstations already equipped to take advantage of conferencing? How many people will be using the connection? Where are the people located?

- Do I already have a LAN in place if there are multiple locations?

- What kind of work do the top 10% of my users do?

- Do I expect my users to become Internet "power users" very quickly?

- How much can I afford to spend on a network connection?

4

Choosing Your Network Provider

The business of providing commercial Internet access got its start in the last few years. Now, there are not-for-profit companies, universities, cooperatives, corporations and projects of corporations, and telephone companies who offer Internet connections. There are individuals running operations out of their garages. These businesses are primarily concerned with installing and servicing the connection from their network to your home, office, or school. They also provide a number of related services such as information systems consulting, administration, and training.

Network providers have made a lot of progress in a few short years to establish a broad base of technical expertise and consistent support for customers. Nonetheless, you should know what to look for in a network provider and how to evaluate the quality of the services they offer. Here are the criteria we will consider:

- Network reliablity

- Network performance

- Network connectivity restrictions

- User services

- Rapport

- Security

- Cost

The goal is to help you ask intelligent questions of network providers about the quality of their service and know when you receive intelligent answers in return.

Network Reliability

"Will I have an Internet connection that works?" It may seem like an obvious question but the most important feature of a good connection is that it works and you stay connected. Your connection must be available to you when you want it and where you want it. Experience and stability are the two best indicators that a network provider can provide a reliable connection. If you repeatedly find that your connection is down, the transport broken, or other failures, you will be very frustrated. Save yourself time and energy by checking on the reliability of the provider's network. As we mention later on, ask for references and use them to ask about the reliability of their connection.

Some network providers are able to offer you service guarantees. A service guarantee usually results in the provider giving you a rebate based on network downtime. When providers are willing to guarantee their services or lose money, you will probably be getting a better connection (or your provider will go out of business quickly!). Service guarantees are usually offered only on dedicated line connections, not on dialup connections.

Network Troubleshooting

Even the best networks fail occasionally and all providers will have outages. The critical factor is how quickly do providers recognize and fix the problems. There are many network tools available to assist providers in monitoring their network and help them recognize a problem.

At a minimum, the provider should have some kind of Simple Network Management Protocol-based (SNMP) monitoring system. SNMP collects performance statistics on various computers throughout the network allowing providers to recognize problems within minutes of occurrence. This can mean that problems get fixed more quickly, perhaps even before you notice them.

However, not all problems can be solved immediately. Good providers have a trouble ticket system in place to track a problem until it is solved. An example of a trouble ticket from NEARnet is shown in Example 4-1. A trouble ticket is simply a record of what the problem is, who is handling it, how it is being handled, and what the time frame is for resolution. These systems are usually electronic and can be checked over the network by the user and the provider.

```
Ticket Number: 1234      Ticket Status:  open
Ticket Type:   unplanned Ticket Source:  e-mail
Ticket Scope:  1site     Site/Line:      XXX
Ticket Owner:  anselmo   Problem Fixer:
Ticket Opened: 05/07/93  18:28  Problem Started:
05/07/93  13:27  User at Small_Stuff reports difficulties mailing to a
company in England, Big_Stuff. Mail is getting to Small_Stuff from the
company, but Small_Stuff is not able to return the mail.
Note: 2  Ed has received the necessary information and will work
05/28/93  12:50  with Small_Stuff personnel.
Note: 4  The problem looks to be with Small_Stuff's sendmail.cf file.
06/24/93  14:57  NEARnet staff will work with Small_Stuff personnel to
get this resolved.
```

Figure 4-1. Sample trouble ticket

Ask about the provider's escalation procedures for trouble tickets. This procedure describes what happens when a problem goes unsolved for a period of time. A ticket that isn't closed immediately (within the day) is usually escalated to higher levels of management until it is closed.

Table 4-1 shows a list of common outages and their causes. While types of outages vary, the downtimes shown can be used as benchmarks. In this figure, power failures at customer sites are the single biggest cause of downtime, while telephone circuit problems are a close second. The sum of all other causes of trouble should be much less than the first two. It pays to check these statistics. If a provider has a lot of unscheduled maintenance or other problems, connections through their networks won't work reliably.

Table 4-1. Network Outages and Their Causes

Outage Type	Cause	Average Downtime
Power Failure	Power Outage	Either seconds or more than four hours
Circuit Failure	Telephone connection down	Four hours
Unscheduled Maintenance	Emergency problem fixing	Less than one hour
Scheduled Maintenance	Planned upgrades or problem fixing	Less than two hours

Table 4-1. Network Outages and Their Causes (Continued)

Outage Type	Cause	Average Downtime
Site Activity	Activity at customer or network site causing outage	Varies
Hardware or Software Problem	Failure of hardware or software	Less than two hours

If an Internet connection is not working for any reason, call or send e-mail (if possible) to the provider to let them know about unsatisfactory performance. Many providers have special telephone lines and e-mail addresses for customer support. Check to see if support is part of normal service or whether you must pay for it. If support is unavailable, choose another provider.

Another way to evaluate a provider's ability to fix a problem is the hours of coverage for their network operations center (NOC). Ask the provider for the hours in which they have NOC coverage. If you want access to the Internet 24 hours per day, seven days per week, then you need to know if there's a procedure for solving problems outside of normal business hours. Remember, support must be available during the times when you most need it.

Network Performance

The parameters for network performance were discussed in Chapter 2. Comparing a provider's statistics with those shown in Chapter 2 will help you assess the quality of the service. Take the example of an individual seeking a dialup account. Both XYZNet and 123Net are asked for price quotes. At the same time, roundtrip times are requested for a site outside of their own networks, to Peoria, for instance. (If you aren't sure how to choose a remote location, ask for roundtrip times for a city 1000 miles away.) The price quotes are similar but XYZNet says the roundtrip time is 350 milliseconds versus 700 milliseconds for 123Net. The choice should be XYZNet, the network with better performance, if all else were equal.

You should not only consider network performance today but in the future. Keeping networks up to date with the latest technology can be expensive and requires careful planning. Ask about the provider's plans to keep the technology current, and look for the following items: planned hardware and software upgrades, modem upgrades, new technology implementations (like ISDN), etc.

Network Connectivity Restrictions

Network performance is also a factor of the provider's network configuration—who is connected to whom, how they are connected, and why. The network provider's connection to the Internet can determine if certain kinds of traffic are subject to restriction.

There are various acceptable use policies (*AUP*) in place. The most notable policy is the NSFNET backbone's acceptable use policy. It restricts traffic on its backbone to research and education uses. Research or education traffic can originate or terminate at educational institutions, research labs, governmental institutions, and commercial businesses. The restriction is on the content of the message or file, not on who is sending the data.

The Commercial Internet Exhange (*CIX*) is an example of one gateway that allows unrestricted (AUP-free) traffic. If using a connection for commerical business transactions is important, be sure that the provider allows, supports, and encourages commercial use and has at least one commercial gateway.

Those Ukrainian sites really knock me out!

One user was trying to reach a site in the Ukraine without success. On investigation, this usThose Ukrainian sites really knock me out!er found that the path died at the NSFNET. A different path through AL-TERnet, a commercial network with a CIX connection, succeeded in reaching the Ukranian site. The reason is perhaps a remnant of the Cold War and the origins of the Internet in the Defense Department. The NSF does not allow traffic to Russia over the NSFNET Service while ALTERnet and the CIX allowed the traffic.

Some of the networks do not allow direct user connections. There are many networks, and larger network providers who will generally have multiple exit paths to other networks. These interconnections are illustrated in Figure 4-2. Check the speed of the exit paths to ensure that they are equivalent or faster than your connection. If you have a particular need, you may want to research the networks you will traverse to make sure there won't be any AUP surprises. Additionally, you should consider where the slowest link in the connection is. You can select the fastest connection in the world, but if you are traversing slower connections all along the way to your destination, your speedy connection will be of no value.

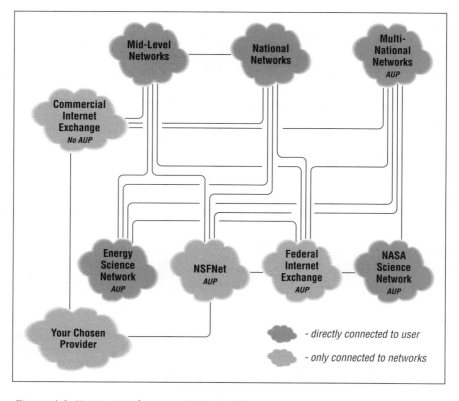

Figure 4-2. How networks are interconnected

User Services

Value-added services are important to many users and help them make effective use of their Internet connection. Some access providers have a user services staff that provides documentation and instruction on how to use the Internet as well as general help. Sometimes, networks refer to user services as network information services or centers (NICs). If a network has a staff dedicated to user services, you are more likely to get the latest information about developments on the Internet. Ask your provider what kinds of specific documentation, instructions, or other help is offered. Some typical functions of a user services group are:

- Outreach: newletters, reports, bulletin boards, announcements
- Training: technical, how to use the Internet, user groups, manuals, books
- Help: answer questions about things to do or how to do them, helpful hints on how to simplify work, finding new resources
- Online Archives: software, manuals, outreach information, network statistics

You may feel that you don't need the services of a dedicated user service staff if you have a lot of experience on the Internet. However, remember that the Internet is a rapidly changing environment and a knowledgeable staff that works to keep you well-informed can be very useful.

Many network providers have set up online help systems to answer common user questions and serve generally as information resources for their clients. Check to see if the provider has one and what kind of information is available on it. If you need beginner information, check for manuals or online documentation. If you are running a large organization, look for statistics and software to assist your local operations.

Some providers make it easy for their customers to access the Internet applications described in Figure 4-3. User interfaces that organize access to the Internet can be of great value if they cut your training costs. In some cases, providers will supply all of the services, such as a USENET newsfeed or Gopher. If they don't, you will have to go to another source to get access to the applications that you want.

Rapport

The underlying success of the Internet is the cooperation of many people throughout the world, working together to build an interoperable network. The provider/client relationships in the Internet are based on the same principle. If a provider is working for you and trying to help you or your business be successful, you will get better service. The provider's responsiveness to questions during the selection process will give clues about your future relationship with the provider. A good rapport with the staff of your provider goes a long way toward keeping you satisfied and fully productive on the Internet.

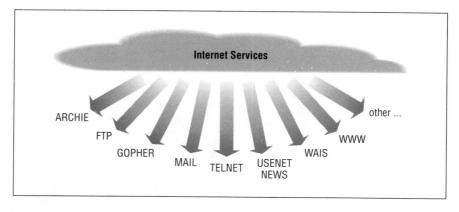

Figure 4-3. Internet services

References

Checking references is the most important thing you can do to ensure that you get the connection you need. You will be surprised at the responses that you can get from references—they will usually be quite frank about their experiences with the provider.

Ask your provider for at least three references. If possible, ask for references who are in the same situation that you are. Look for references with the same kind of computers, a similar number of users, and in the same industry as you are. Then call them. Ask them what they like best about the provider. Ask them what their biggest problems have been. Ask them if they feel that the provider is working in their best interest.

If you don't think the references you have received are bona fide, get a copy of the provider's customer list and call a few on your own. If you mistrust your potential provider that much, think about finding another provider.

You can also use online forums such as USENET to learn about an Internet provider's virtues and shortcomings. You might ask others to share their experience with you. You'll get more information than you can imagine.

Security Issues

Security threats are real once a connection to the Internet is established. The "Site Security Handbook" says: "The Internet allows the electronic equivalent of the thief who looks for open windows and doors; now a person can check hundreds of machines for vulnerabilities in a few hours." While security is usually not a big deal for individuals with dialup connections, both small and large businesses should work with their provider to understand what kind of preventive measures are appropriate. If security is a serious concern of yours, present the providers with a site security plan and ask about preventive measures for ensuring against unwanted intrusions.

Figure 4-4 shows various techniques available to secure your Internet connection. Two of the most widely used techniques are firewalls or access lists. Both provide the same functionality. With firewalls, a computer is set up between your internal network and the Internet. All traffic flow diverts through it. With access lists, you build inbound and outbound traffic requirements directly in the router. In both cases, you can do such security as limiting inbound FTPs, TELNETs, etc., requiring special login for outbound traffic, denying particular addresses either inbound or outbound, etc.

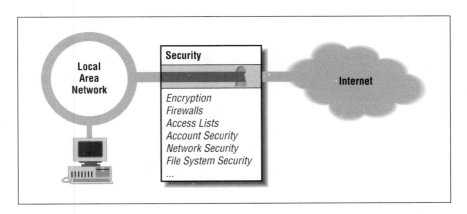

Figure 4-4. Security measures that protect a LAN from the Internet

In addition to securing the connection, ask about the provider's procedure for ensuring that data is not being viewed, discussed, or otherwise disseminated without the knowledge of the sender or receiver. This procedure should include handling data about statistics or usage patterns.

Cost

Prices vary considerably among providers. High prices do not necessarily guarantee better service. Lower prices do not always mean you are getting a good deal. Free connections sometimes end up costing you more than you anticipated.

There are no hard and fast rules about what you should pay for a link. The best idea is to figure out which of the criteria listed at the end of this chapter and in Chapters 5 and 6 are most important to you. For quotes or pricelists, compare networks against each other. If you can get an equivalent service for less money, choose it. Be sure that you understand exactly what you are getting for your money.

Don't forget that equipment can be a large part, or the majority, of the startup costs. Some routers may cost $10,000 or more. You may have the option of renting the equipment from the Internet vendor. Renting may make sense if you can't afford the equipment up front, but it usually costs more in the long run. One advantage of renting from the vendor is that if something goes wrong with the equipment, they are responsible. If you own the equipment, you may get "finger-pointing" instead of a fix for the problem. Even if renting costs you more, the money may be worth it if things go wrong with the connection. You will probably have to learn how to configure the equipment on your own if you buy it. This gives you more control over its use, but you also get into situations where you have to prove that the problem is not with your equipment.

Budgeting for an Internet connection is critical. While Internet connections can be inexpensive, they can scale up quickly. Ensure that you have allotted money in your budget to pay for the annual cost. In businesses or large organizations, the purchase of an Internet connection goes through an approval process, sometimes taking months. Chapter 5 provides a chart for evaluating dialup connection costs. Chapter 6 provides a chart for evaluating dedicated line connection costs. These will help individuals, small businesses, and large organizations to understand the total cost of a connection and budget accordingly.

Most of the providers have a contract or agreement that must be signed prior to connection. Large organizations and other businesses should carefully review the terms and conditions in the agreement. Individuals should review the agreement, too.

Free Connections

You can get a free connection if you know someone who will connect you. Be cautious. It could be the deal of a lifetime or it could be a disaster. You can get into all kinds of trouble; consider your tolerance level for long or nonexistent installation schedules, or waiting for problems with your link to be solved. There may be restrictions on your use; you may be limited to specific hours of the day. A site may tolerate you until you begin to create significant traffic or use up noticeable amounts of space on their disk. The point is that you are not a paying customer, and your privileges can be cut off.

You can get really great connections for free, but be prepared for the day when the connection is no longer free or is disconnected suddenly. If you have correctly evaluated your needs, you will know if a free connection is for you. Not everyone can find one, and not everyone should get one even if they can. While free connections may work for small businesses and individuals, I don't recommend them for large organizations, unless there is no other alternative

Friendly Connections

Some sites may offer to sell you a piece of their link. This can be a smart way to save money, but, as with free connections, you must approach this kind of connection with caution. Investigate the network performance and reliability of the site. There are many variations of this kind of offer: a shared link within a building, backdoor connections discussed in Chapter 6, and dialup into a dedicated site connection.

I have heard horror stories from sites who have paid for unusable connections through other organizations. One site connected to a large organization whose local network was so congested that it was almost impossible to use. The site's Internet traffic had to pass through that local network, a performance factor they had not considered when purchasing the link. Evaluate your needs properly and you will know whether you can "afford" this type of connection.

Finding a Network Provider

There are a number of places to find providers of Internet connections. At this time, there are over 100 Internet provider businesses and hundreds more that fall under the categories described above. While we have provided a listing of providers in the appendices, we can also point you to several sources so that you can get an updated list.

There are a number of online lists available for your use. The PDIAL list, compiled by Peter Kaminski, covers dialup connections. The Dlist, compiled for this book, covers dedicated connections. Both are available by FTP and e-mail and are updated regularly. They are included in Appendices A and B along with instructions on how to get updates.

There are a number of organizations that network providers join for camaraderie and information sharing. CIX and FARNET are two of the most popular. They can provide a listing of member networks upon request. These listings can be handy when looking for a provider. CIX is a trade association which focuses on commercial Internetworking issues. Its membership consists of 18 networks. You can receive the CIX listing by calling 303-482-2150 or by sending e-mail to info@cix.org. FARNET is a membership organization that promotes research and education networking in the U.S. Its membership consists of 35 networks. You can receive the FARNET listing by calling 617-890-5120 or by sending e-mail to breeden@farnet.org.

Changing Providers

The business of providing Internet access is changing and competition is increasing. You want to consider the ability of your network provider to remain competitive, and you also want to be able to change providers if you can get a better value from another provider. If a provider asks that you sign a multiyear contract for their services, be sure that you understand your options before making that kind of committment.

The length of time a provider has been in business is not always relevant in determining the viability of a provider. The knowledge base of the provider, their reputation, their ability to satisfy customers, their ability to upgrade, and their ability to be innovative with new services are all better criteria for judging whether the service will remain viable.

It is expensive to change providers. For individuals or small businesses using dialup accounts, it's like moving from one apartment to another. You will have to send a change of address to colleagues, and there might be a lag time while you make a transition from the old to the new provider. This inconvenience should not keep you from changing if the change will improve your connectivity. As a person who just changed her e-mail address, I can testify that the transition is a process that will take a while. Find out if your old provider will put a forwarding address on your account. Or keep your old account for a month or two with an automatic reply stating your new address.

Medium or large organizations will usually have to get a new telephone link and pay substantial installation charges to move their connection. Again, this should not stop you from changing if you feel that your current service is unsatisfactory or the new service will offer significant benefits. See if you can convince the new provider to make some concessions on installation fees to ease the financial burden of the change. Make sure you have evaluated all the steps necessary to change before notifying your current provider. In rare circumstances, the provider may try to hinder your transition.

The best thing is, of course, to make the right choice at the start. Chapters 5 and 6 will help you do that.

General Checklist for Choosing a Network Provider

Reliability & Performance

Is the end-to-end roundtrip time greater than 500 milliseconds?

What is the local roundtrip time for connections like the one you want?

Can I get a service guarantee? What is it?

What are typical outages and how long do they last?

What kind of monitoring system does the provider use?

Is there a trouble ticket system? What are problem resolution procedures? What are the escalation procedures?

How do you tell the provider that something is broken? Is there a phone and/or e-mail address for trouble reporting? How will you know when the problem is fixed?

What are the NOC hours of coverage? What happens if the NOC is not covered when you have a problem?

Restrictions

Are there any restrictions on how I use the network?

Are there any acceptable use policies?

How do you route commerical traffic?

What other networks do you connect to directly? At what speeds?

If you have specific data destinations identified, will you traverse AUP networks? What is the slowest connection in the path?

User Services

Can I use all of the Internet tools and services I need?

Does the provider have a User Services department? What do they do? How much does it cost—extra or included?

What extra services does the provider offer? How much do they cost?

Rapport

Is the provider working for me?

Am I getting honest, straight answers to my questions?

Will I continue to get these after I have made my selection?

Security

Am I concerned about unwanted intrusions on my computers?

What techniques does the provider recommend or support for security at your site?

What are the procedures for ensuring that my data is kept private?

Viability

Does the provider plan to upgrade to the newest technologies when I want them?

What is the contract or agreement like? Can I live with the terms and conditions?

References

Get at least three references and call them.

If you can, check online in newsgroups or mailing lists.

Cost

Do I know what I am getting for my fees?

Do I have a budget for a connection?

Free Connections

Is a free connection right for my needs?

Do I know anyone who will give me one?

Friendly Connections

Is a piece of someone else's connection the right link for me?

Have I used the evaluation criteria here to ensure that I am getting a high quality connection?

Finding Providers

Have I gotten the most recent listing of providers?

Do I need to get additional lists?

5

Selecting Dialup Connections

Dialup connections are appropriate for individuals and small businesses with low- to moderate-impact applications and budgets. Dialup connections vary widely in performance and price, so it's important to know what your needs are before you start looking at providers. If you are going to use your connection primarily for fun, you can put up with some performance quirks and save money. If you are going to use your connection for business purposes, you need a more stable connection.

What Kind of Connections Are Available?

There are two types of dialup connections: online accounts or dialup IP links. Dialup IP links are usually described by the particular protocol they are running: either Serial Line Internet Protocol (SLIP) or the more advanced Point to Point Protocol (PPP).

Both types of connections can give you a lot of things to do on the network. If you are starting your Internet adventure as an individual, an online account is easy to access and less expensive. If your usage is heavy, or if you have several people on a local area network (LAN), a SLIP or PPP connection becomes necessary.

If you have an an online account, you connect from your own computer using a telephone line and a modem, just as you would connect to a bulletin board. An online account is one step removed from full Internet connectivity, though, and has some important limitations. If you have a

SLIP or PPP account, you also connect through a modem over a phone line, but your computer runs TCP/IP software to talk the TCP/IP protocol. A SLIP or PPP actually puts your computer on the network, and gives you full Internet access.

Online Accounts

An online account is an account on a host computer that's connected to the Internet. To the host, your computer looks like a character-based terminal, and your communications software provides terminal emulation. (VT100 is a popular terminal type supported by most systems and most communications software.) When you dial into the host computer, you must log in and supply a password to get into your account.

Many of the public access providers run UNIX, where online accounts are referred to as shell accounts. (The shell is a program that you interact with by typing commands.) You may see a UNIX prompt or you may go into a custom menu-based interface. One way or another, you can usually send and receive electronic mail. Most online accounts let you use programs like Gopher, WAIS, WWW, TELNET, FTP, or any other program available on the host. Some don't. All of the providers listed in Appendix B offer at least outbound TELNET and FTP.

The drawback of an online account is that it takes two steps to get data onto your machine. You must download the data first to the host, and then to your own computer (see Figure 5-1). The FTP utility (File Transfer Protocol) is commonly used to retrieve data from the Internet and put it on the host. Then, to download it from the host to your machine, you can use one of the standard file transfer protocols like kermit, xmodem, ymodem, or zmodem. Another way is to use the screen capture feature (most communications software packages include this) to copy data as you view it on your own computer. FTP or other Internet-based applications do not run on your computer, as they depend upon the underlying support of the TCP/IP protocols to work.

Now, this "double download" can be a benefit in disguise. It lets you retrieve big data files (that might not even fit on your own disk) and look at them on the host. You can decide if you really want to the file on your local machine after you view it—you might copy only the piece of the file that you want. Downloading to the host can save the disk space on your own computer. (Of course, you may be paying for the amount of disk space you use on the host.)

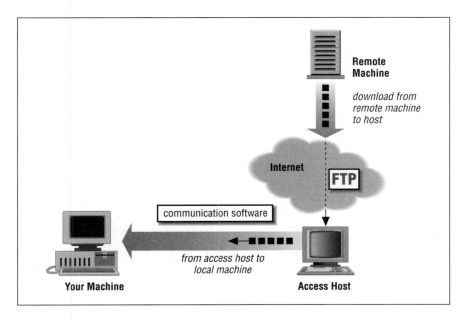

Figure 5-1. Double download requires transferring file via FTP from the network and then downloading it to local machine using Xmodem or other communications

Because you read e-mail, USENET News, etc. on the host machine, you are doing all of your data processing while you are online (connected to the host). Keep this in mind if you are paying by the minute for the time you spend online.

An online account can be useful if you travel a lot. You can log in to the host machine from different computers and different locations. Your special files, network addresses, or software will be available to you. For example, if you're traveling with a portable computer, consider a provider with an 800 number or nationwide local access numbers that you can use to dial into your online account.

Online accounts work well at any speeds up to the current modem standards. (See Chapter 2 for a listing of common modem standards.) Higher speed modems or different access options (as opposed to regular telephone lines) allow your computer screen to update more quickly and also help keep your online time to a minimum. You may pay a premium for access via a higher speed modem.

Online accounts work well for individuals or small businesses who want a simple, low cost access to the Internet.

Equipment Required

Figure 5-2 shows the equipment needed for a typical online account connection. At your site, you need a computer, a modem, communication software, and a regular phone line. (Many modems come with free software.)

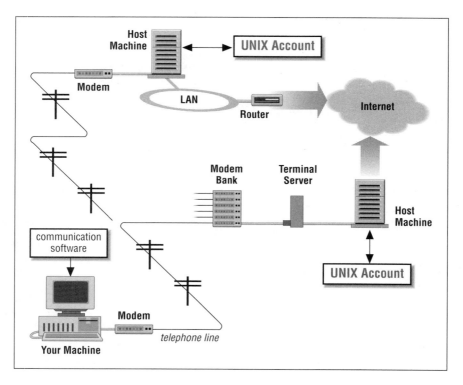

Figure 5-2. A dialup connection requires a modem on your end and a phone line that connects to a modem connected to the host or to a terminal server

On the supplier's side, you either go directly into the host computer, or you connect to a modem bank and then to a terminal server. A terminal server is a device that allows for multiple modem connections into the network. Most larger providers have a terminal server.

If you do go through a terminal server, you may need to perform a TELNET session to log in to the host. This is simple to do, especially if your communications software supports scripts. With a script, you go through the motions once, then the next time you log in the scripts remember where you went and how you got there.

If not included with your modem, communications software is available as freeware, shareware, and through commercial sources. Common packages are:

- Macintosh: ZTerm, Microphone Pro, VersaTerm, MacIntercomm, SmartCom

- PC with DOS: Telemate, Telix, Procomm

- PC with Windows: Procomm Plus

Interface

Don't overlook what you see once you connect to the host. The user interface must be something you can use productively. Extras such as good e-mail and news interfaces, and custom menu-driven systems can have significant value if they save you time and improve your productivity. Check for software that simplifies your access to the Internet. Software programs can vary from command driven e-mail readers (you type in commands rather than use menus or icons) to graphical user interfaces (GUIs) that work like the operating system of your computer.

Figure 5-3 shows an example of CERFnet's menu system that makes an online account easier to use.

```
Internet  Compass            Main Menu                        v1.0
      A          Account Tools - User Account Tools
      C          CERFnet Info  - CERFnet Info and News
      F          Files         - File Transfers
      G          Games         - Electronic Entertainment
      I          Internet      - Internet Search Tools
      M          Mail          - Electronic Mail
      N          News          - USENET News
      T          Telnet        - Remote Login to Other Systems
      U          UNIX Shell    - Escape to UNIX Shell Commands
      Q          Quit          - Exit
      ?          Help          - Help using Internet Compass
                     Enter Selection
```

Figure 5-3. CERFnet's Internet compass screen

Some providers stick to a basic prompt like:

```
nic%
```

Some have made it easier to navigate the network by simpifying basic functions. Others have made it very easy for you by providing an extensive help system online. The basic prompt can make you feel somewhat ignorant if you have had little or no prior experience with computer systems. With a good desk reference book, like Ed Krol's *The Whole Internet Users Guide and Catalog,* you can get along with a prompt, although it may seem challenging at times. If you are allergic to manuals or want to do as much as possible without one, look for a provider that has a menu interface or a good help system.

Installation

Presuming you have the correct equipment, installation of an online account is simple and quick. It is usually a matter of signing an agreement and receiving a telephone number to call, a login ID and password. Some providers make it easy to sign up online, allowing immediate access to the Internet.

Additional Considerations

Network performance should be taken into account when choosing an online account. You have to be able to get access to an available modem line on the provider end, and you don't want frequent busy signals. Ask them how many modems are available. How often are they all busy? When will the provider add adntitial modems? Answering these questions will translate back to network availability—will you be able to log in when you want to? If you want to be sure that you always have immediate access, some providers have dedicated modem connections, which means that the modem line on their end is there for your exclusive use.

The amount of disk space allotted to each online account on the host computer varies considerably. This can present a real problem if upgrade options are not available. If disk space is limited on the host, you may not be able to transfer files or store e-mail. During the preparation of this book, I had to increase my disk space allotment to handle the volume of file transfer underway. Some providers have a shared storage area available for temporary transfers, while doing double downloading. Find out how much disk space you will be allotted and what it will cost to expand it if necessary. One megabyte of space is the minimum you want. Ask if a temporary area is available for use.

The total number of simultaneous users on the host computer can also be a performance factor. If a supplier tries to support too many simultaneous users, the host computer slows down, causing delays to users doing routine tasks.

Cost

Most service providers have flat rates or hourly usage charges. There are networks who have a flat rate for a fixed amount of hours or for usage within certain hours. Evaluate your needs thoroughly then compare costs. If you'll be using your connection during evening and weekend hours, check for special rates for off hours.

Be careful when evaluating different costs. Some online accounts won't allow use of anything but e-mail and USENET News. If you want to use Gopher, TELNET, etc. you have to upgrade to a higher priced account. In order to correctly evaluate cost versus benefit, ask what applications are included.

Figure 5-4 helps you compare costs among providers. To make the best cost comparison, estimate the time you will spend online. Light Internet users typically are online from five to 15 hours per month. Medium Internet users are online 20 to 50 hours per month. If you are a heavy Internet user, don't worry about how much time you are online; find a connection for a fixed price.

The comparison in Figure 5-5 assumes that a user would connect during business hours, Monday through Friday, for one hour per day. In comparing the five networks, we used the criteria listed at the end of this chapter. XYZNet, the cheapest, had busy signals over a period of time when I wanted to log in to check disk space allotments. It was disqualified due to lack of adequate dialup facilities.

All of the listed parameters were taken into account, using "local access" telephone numbers. After factoring in the toll charge from the "local" numbers, there were surprising results. At first glance, the apparent low cost solution was ABCNet with a monthly charge of $20 for unlimited usage. Unfortunately, its "local number" toll charges added up to a whopping $11.49 per hour. Instead of being the lowest cost solution, it was the most expensive choice. 123Net the winner even though billing was done

Cost Comparison - Online Account

Service Provider	Setup Fee	Fixed Monthly Charge	Hours Included	Extra Hourly Charge	Other Costs	Toll Charge Incurred	Estimated Monthly Cost
1							
2							
3							
4							
5							
6							
7							
8							
9							

Assumed Time On-line: _____

Comments:

Figure 5-4. Cost comparison—online accounts

Cost Comparison - Online Account							
Service Provider	Setup Fee	Fixed Monthly Charge	Hours Included	Extra Hourly Charge	Other Costs	Toll Charge Incurred (per hr.)	Estimated Monthly Cost
1 XYZNet	10	15	unlim.	0	0	0	15.00
2 123net	50	20	0	5	0	0.63	132.60
3 ABCnet	15	20	unlim.	0	0	11.49	249.80
4 TollFreenet	25	25	0	8.5	0	0	195.00
5 X.25Net	0	6	0	11.5	0	0	236.00

Assumption: 20 hours per month of online time (1 hour per day)

Figure 5-5. Sample cost comparison—online account

on hourly usage. TollFreeNet was the runner up. X.25Net had a hefty hourly charge for access to a 2400 bps modem and was thus disqualified.

SLIP and PPP CONNECTIONS

With a SLIP or PPP connection, your own computer has a full Internet connection capable of sending and receiving data from other computers on the network. You can run networking applications (such as e-mail, FPT, WAIS, and WWW) locally on your computer. Another benefit of a SLIP or PPP connection is the fact that you can open up multiple sessions, allowing simultaneous interaction with different computers on the Internet. In one window you could be running an FTP session while you are using Gopher in another. You can set up your system so that e-mail can come directly to it. The option to use your own domain name is an important consideration.

SLIP and PPP should be used with modem capable of at least 9600 bps, with 14.4 kbps preferred. A SLIP or PPP connection can have difficulties with certain types of compression. Check with your supplier for recommendations regarding specific settings for your modem.

One of the drawbacks of a SLIP or PPP connection is the initial difficulty in configuring the software. I have spoken to many frustrated users during the setup process who have been ready to give up after a week or two of problems. In the end, they usually were successful in connecting. In order to use a dialup IP connection, plan on having to learn more about TCP/IP and configuration issues. A lot can be said for good documentation and technical support, and a good friend who can walk you through the process.

Equipment Required

Figure 5-6 shows the hardware needed in a SLIP or PPP connection. TCP/IP software runs on the computers accessing the router, and the SLIP or PPP software runs on the router itself. There are many implementations of SLIP and PPP software available. Table 5-1 lists a few commerical packages. The support provided by SLIP software vendors and the improved reliablity of commercial implementations are often worth the money spent ($100 – $700).

Table 5-1. Commerical Slip Software

System	Package	Company
PC Dos and windows	Chameleon	Netmanage
PC Dos and windows	SuperTCP	Frontier Tech Corporation.
Macintosh	Versatilities	Synergy Software
Macintosh	MacSLIP	Trisoft
Unix	Morningstar PPP/SLIP	Morning Star Technologies

Another option for SLIP and PPP connections is a SLIP/PPP router. This setup works better for LANs because each computer doesn't have to have a modem. (Also, you don't have to configure your own SLIP or PPP software.) The router handles the dialup setup for you, which means that except for a dialing delay while the computer "talks" to the router, the connection appears the same as a dedicated line.

A number of hardware vendors are building routers which include modems and SLIP or PPP software. Two examples are the NetHopper from Rockwell International and the NetBlazer from Telebit. They can be easily attached to a computer for a simple Internet connection. Many of the network providers will sell or rent the routers. They will usually

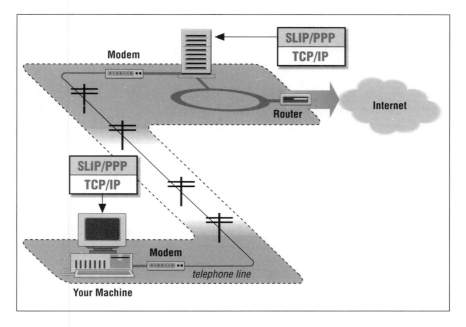

Figure 5-6. A SLIP/PPP connection allows your machine to be part of a local area network

configure the router to work with their network, providing an easy solution for Internet connectivity. A router solution is practical for small businesses. This solution is still expensive for individuals ($1500 list) when compared to a software plus modem configuration.

Installation

As noted, the installation of SLIP and PPP can be a painful process. This can be minimized by working with a knowledgable provider who will provide technical help and moral support during the installation. In order to set up a SLIP or PPP account, you should have the following information available:

• TCP/IP address (from the provider)

• Domain name if wanted (from Internet Domain Registry service at rs.internic.net)

• Domain name and address of the primary and secondary name server (from the provider)

• Subnet mask (from the provider)

- Size of the maximum receivable unit
- MRU (from the provider)
- SLIP or PPP software or router
- TCP/IP software

Getting signed up for a SLIP or PPP account is simple and quick. It will usually involve some kind of agreement or contact, especially if you are using a router from the provider.

Options

Deciding between SLIP and PPP is important. Another SLIP option called CSLIP is also available. CSLIP, compressed SLIP, compresses the IP address information in data, thus making file transfers faster. If you will be doing many large file transfers, you should consider CSLIP. A provider's equipment will usually support only one option: either SLIP, CSLIP, or PPP. If you feel strongly about using one type of software, ask the provider if that option is available.

Another option to track is the availability of a static IP address. This will allow you to have your own domain name. Some providers use dynamic addressing which will keep you from using your own domain name. If you are going to dialup different SLIP servers and you have a static IP address, you will need a different IP address for each server and have to change your configuation.

Cost

Most service providers have flat rates for SLIP and PPP services. A few have hourly usage charges. The jump in cost from an online account to SLIP or PPP can be large. The flat-rate services are typically ten times the cost of online accounts. If you'll use your connection during evening and weekend hours and purchase an hourly rate service, check for specials on rates for off-hours.

Figure 5-7 helps you compare costs among providers for SLIP or PPP connections. Remember to estimate the time you will spend online: light (five to 15 hours per month), medium (20 to 50 hours per month), or heavy (above 50 hours per month).

The comparison in Figure 5-8 assumes that a user would connect during business hours, Monday through Friday, for two hours per day. Four

SLIP/PPP Cost Comparison

Service Provider	Setup Fee	Fixed Monthly Charge	Hours Included	Other Costs	Toll Charge Incurred	Estimated Monthly Cost
1						
2						
3						
4						
5						
6						
7						
8						
9						

Assumed Time On-line: _____

Comments:

Figure 5-7. SLIP/PPP cost comparison

networks were compared using the criteria listed at the end of this chapter. As in the comparison of online accounts, the hidden extra cost of toll charges to "local" dialup numbers ended up as the overriding cost consideration. XYZNet, with a fixed monthly cost and a relatively inexpensive toll charge, was the winner. 123Net came in second, with hourly usage charges. If usage was to drop by 15 minutes per day, XYZNet and 123Net would cost the same. If usage was to increase substantially, XYZNet would be the obvious choice.

SLIP/PPP Cost Comparison						
Service Provider	Setup Fee	Fixed Monthly Charge	Hours Included	Other Costs	Toll Charge Incurred (per hr.)	Estimated Monthly Cost
1 XYZNet	10	175	unlim.	0	1.45	173.00
2 123net	50	10	0	0	1.45	318.00
3 ABCnet	15	150	unlim.	0	11.49	379.80
4 TollFreenet	15	10	0	0	0	360.00
5						

Assumption: 40 hours per month of online time (2 hours per day)

Figure 5-8. Sample SLIP/PPP cost comparison

Access Options

In addition to regular telephone lines, there are two other popular methods for dialup access: ISDN and X.25. In both cases, network providers need to have special connections installed to support access via these methods. Another consideration for access is the availability of local or toll-free access numbers.

ISDN

One alternative access method for dialup is the Integrated Services Digital Network (ISDN). ISDN lets you use a special telephone line for data and voice simultaneously, which can be cost effective. ISDN offers higher speeds over a digital link and a better quality connection than with modems. To use an ISDN connection, you need a piece of equipment that substitutes for the modem. Some workstations have ISDN equipment built into the computer. Otherwise, the ISDN interface device has a price tag between $1000 and $1500, a major step up from inexpensive modems.

ISDN has been slowly spreading throughout the US, and not everybody can get it. If you are not near a major city or your phone company has older equipment, you may have to wait years before ISDN is available. (Your phone company should have a number to call for the ISDN "deployment schedule" for your area.)

An alternative that is currently available is called Switched 56k (SW56k). This is a switched data-only service that runs at 56 kbps ("Basic Rate Interface" ISDN lets you run up to 128 kbps of data or voice). It is very much like a phone call in that it uses a normal looking phone number and takes a little while to connect (whereas ISDN connections are very quick to set up). SW56k requires special wiring and uses different lines than voice lines (whereas ISDN uses normal voice lines). It is a metered service, meaning you pay by the minute (or second), and long distance costs more than local calls. If you are using it for an Internet connection, you should use equipment that only dials up when there is data to send. If the SW56k service is used often enough, there is a point at which it becomes more cost-effective to have a dedicated 56K connection (DDS) line. The biggest advantage of SW56k is that you can call multiple locations using phone numbers, while a dedicated service ties you to a single location. This type of service would be perfect for a print shop or service bureau where customers use SW56k (or ISDN) to submit printing jobs.

ISDN offers a data rate of 128 kbps, adding together two 64 kbps channels (called "bearer channels" in ISDN-speak). Each channel can carry voice or data, so you could have a voice call on one channel and a 64 kbps data connection on the other. Sites with ISDN can usually call sites that use SW56k, but their data rate would get chopped from 128 kbps to 56 kbps. Some phone companies are offering "single line" ISDN (possibly called "IS") which is a single 56 kbps connection. You might encounter another situation where each ISDN channel is only 56 kbps, yielding a combined data rate of 112 kbps. Check with your local phone company for their ISDN offering.

X.25

The other dialup option is an X.25 network. With an X.25 connection, you need the same equipment as you would with a normal dialup connection. While you may think of an X.25 connection as a regular telephone line, you may notice slower performance, such as a delay in seeing what you have typed. Popular X.25 networks are TYMNET and SPRINTNet. X.25 is not recommended for a SLIP or PPP connection. The additional routing information added to normal TCP/IP means X.25 links have dismal performance. However, modem connections using X.25 are quite affordable at this time.

When is long distance cheaper than a local call?

If you look at the dollars per byte tranferred, X.25 networks tend to be more expensive than direct dial long distance or 800 number services. The reason for this is twofold. First, X.25 is usually only 2400 bps so it will take longer to transfer data. Second, you are paying for two connections, once to the X.25 provider and once to the Internet provider. It is easy to pay $10 per hour for 2400 bps service, a high price for a slow connection.

Toll-free versus Local Access Numbers

Finding a local phone number at the speed you want may save you large amounts of money. Some Internet providers also offer toll-free 800 numbers and bundle the cost of your call in their total charges to you for the Internet connection. While the provider's charges for such toll-free numbers may look expensive at first glance, they may save you money if you don't have a local phone number to call. Toll-free numbers are especially useful if you travel a great deal and don't want to remember (or look up) the local telephone numbers. When you are comparing the cost of 800 number service with local service, check for any toll charges you may incur from dialing the provider's closest local telephone line. You can get rates from the front of your phone book or by calling your telephone company. I was very surprised when I learned that a call from my home to my local node, a distance of 15 miles, cost $2.50 per hour. Of course, if you are not charged by message units for a local call, and your connection is local, then you can stay logged in all the time for a fixed monthly cost.

Comparing Dialup Options

You should consider whether you can upgrade from an online account to a SLIP or PPP connection. This is important if you anticipate expanding your organization. Some providers have interchangable accounts, where you can have either type of connection. Some require different methods of access between the two. Check to see if there will be additional fees if you upgrade from an online account to a SLIP or PPP connection.

Find out when the provider does scheduled maintenance of the terminal server or host computer. Make sure that it is not down during a time when you need Internet access.

Dialup Account Checklist of Questions

Online Accounts

Do I have the required equipment configuration?

Do I need or want the added benefit of a menu-driven system to simplify online access?

How often does the provider experience busy signals?

What is their procedure for adding additional modems?

How much disk space do I get? How does this compare with other providers?

Is the host computer congested?

Is there a local number to dial?

Is a toll-free number an option?

Is there ISDN access?

Is there X.25 access?

Can I upgrade to SLIP for no additional charge?

When is maintenance scheduled on the terminal server and modems? Host computer?

What is the real cost of the connection? (See Figure 5-4).

SLIP or PPP Accounts

Do I want to connect one computer or a LAN?

Do I have the required equipment configuration including software?

Do I want to learn more about TCP/IP?

Do I have the time to set up a SLIP or PPP connection? If not, can I get help from the provider?

Do I have a domain name?

Does the provider do static or dynamic addressing?

How often does the provider experience busy signals?

What is their procedure for adding additional modems?

How much disk space do I get? How does this compare with other providers?

Is the host computer congested?

Is there a local number to dial?

Is a toll-free number an option?

Is there ISDN access?

Is there X.25 access?

When is maintenance scheduled on the terminal server and modems?

What is the real cost of the connection? (See Figure 5-7).

In this chapter:
• Overview of
  Dedicated Line
  Connections
• Dedicated Line
  Checklist of
  Questions

6

Selecting
Dedicated Line
Connections

Dedicated lines are appropriate for sites with a large number of users or with a lot of data to offer to other users on the Internet. Because of the cost, a dedicated line is usually too expensive for individuals or small businesses. A dedicated line connects a local area network(s) to the Internet. All of the users at the site can have access to the connection if they are connected to the LAN. In most cases, it makes little sense to connect less than a LAN through a dedicated line. A large organization or a small business can benefit in particular from having a full-time, full-power connection.

Overview of Dedicated Line Connections

There are many types of dedicated line connections, but they all have a few things in common: local area networks are connected to a router; a dedicated telephone line is installed for access; a lot of work is required to set up your site.

Figure 6-1 shows the most typical dedicated line connection. At your site, you need at least one computer running TCP/IP software on the LAN. The LAN is attached to a router that hooks up to the telephone link. The telephone link consists of a digital telephone line with a CSU/DSU (a digital conversion device) at each end.   (This is different from the modem, SLIP, or PPP line.) The telephone link is hooked into a router/-gateway at the provider's end of the circuit. The speed of the telephone link can be from 9.6 kilobits-per-second to 45 megabits-per-second. Usually, the price of the link is a fixed monthly cost based on the speed you choose.

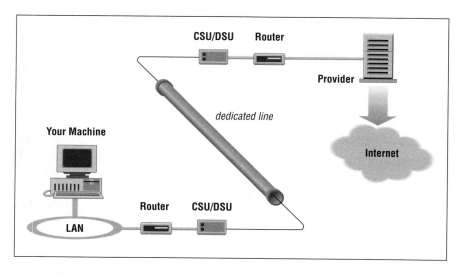

Figure 6-1. Dedicated line connection between two networks

A dedicated line connection can substitute software for a router at your site. The rest of the connection remains the same. This configuration may save money since a router is not used. It is appropriate for sites with a low number of users, but is not recommended for large organizations. Future growth should be kept in mind when selecting this option. Time and time again, people underestimate their growth plans and end up paying more because of it. Plan to grow gracefully.

There are also other kinds of telephone circuits. You can choose an analog dedicated line that involves placing modems instead of CSU/DSUs at each end of the telephone line. You can also choose some newer transport technologies which may change the hardware necessary in the connection. Some of the newer technologies, described below, require special hardware and software to function properly.

The Circuits

The telecommunications links in Internet connections are usually provided by telephone companies or others who have wiring available. Examples of companies that provide the circuits are local Bell Operating Companies like Pacific Bell, long distance phone companies like AT&T, MCI, and Sprint, and specialized telephone companies like Cable and Wireless, WilTel, and Metropolitan Fiber Systems. Most of the Internet service providers "rent" circuits from one of these types of companies. Table 6-1 shows typical speeds for telephone circuits that can be installed.

The cost for analog and digital telephone circuits depends on the distance between the two sites to be connected. This means that the distance between your site and the provider's point of presence (POP) will determine the cost of the circuit.

Table 6-1. Speeds of Different Types of Connections.

Type	Speed
Analog	9.6, 14.4, 19.2 kbps
Digital	56 kbps, 1.544 mbps (T1), 45 mbps, subrated T1 (up to 1.544 mbps in increments of 64 kbps)
Frame Relay	56 kbps, 128, 256, 512 kbps
SMDS	56 kbps, 1.544 mbps, 4 mbps, 10 mbps

Different technologies employed by the telecommunications industry allow different choices for circuits on the Internet. Traditional choices have been analog and digital point-to-point circuits. Alternatives like SMDS (Switched Multimegabit Digital Service), Asynchronous Transfer Mode (ATM), and frame relay are emerging as efficient and cost effective choices. These circuits have fixed prices based on guaranteed bandwidth, not on the distance between two points. In Internet connections, these newer digital circuits allow both access to the public Internet and use of the circuit for private connections via permanent virtual circuits (PVC). PVCs are software based circuits that act as private lines between sites for specialized individual applications. (For example, you might use such a private virtual circuit to route additional, non-Internet data such as Apple-Talk or Novell IPX network packets to your remote sites. Incidentally, you can do the same kind of thing with a leased line. Note, however, that you can't route such packets over the Internet itself without specialized software for encapsulating the foreign network packets within IP packets). Since they are software based, PVCs can be added and deleted quickly as individual applications vary. This feature makes the Internet connection more valuable since it can be used for more than just Internet access.

When installing a circuit, strict schedules are followed by the telephone companies. Usually, a circuit takes a minimum of 17 working days (3.5 weeks) for installation. Internet providers work their installation schedules around those of the circuit installers.

Equipment Required

One of the most important items to determine, especially when comparing costs, is who supplies the hardware in the connection. There are providers who supply, maintain, and upgrade all of the equipment in the connection up to and including the router at your site. Other providers insist that you supply and maintain everything up to the CSU/DSU at their site. You can find every variation in between. Provider selection should be based on the technical expertise of the local staff and the importance of a service guarantee to your site. Providers can only guarantee connections that they manage and maintain, so don't expect a guarantee if you are providing your own hardware.

The hardware required in the typical Internet connection is shown in Figure 6-1 on Page 68 and includes:

Router at your site

- CSU/DSU at your site
- Cables to connect router to CSU/DSU
- Telephone circuit
- CSU/DSU at provider's site
- Port on router at provider's site

There are many companies that build routers: Cisco, Wellfleet, and Proteon are some you may have heard mentioned. CSU/DSU companies are too numerous to list. If you are planning to supply your own equipment, get the recommendations of your Internet provider so you don't end up with something that is incompatible.

The software required in a typical Internet connection, usually supplied by the site, includes:

- TCP/IP
- Mail transport
- Domain name system
- FTP
- Telnet
- Other client software like Gopher, WAIS, etc.

Software exists for almost any type of computer on the planet. UNIX system software generally includes all of this software. If you have to get your own software, you will find that some implementations are free in the public domain and some are commercial packages. Internet providers will usually give you a list of software they recommend. Or you can find another site with a similar configuration and talk to the site administrator for advice.

Installation and Maintenance

Preparing for a dedicated line connection is complicated and is most appropriate for sites that already have a network administrator. With a dedicated line, all of the computers on your network must be ready and secure enough to attach to a public network like the Internet. You have to set up software programs that let you communicate with others on the Internet. And you have to configure your computers with appropriate addresses and routing. These tasks take knowledge, skill, time, and planning, and get more complicated as your network grows.

We don't have space in this book to detail all of these tasks. What we try to do here is simply to give pointers for your technical staff to investigate. Some of the books in the bibliography (such as *TCP/IP Network Administration* by Craig Hunt, and *DNS and BIND* by Paul Albitz and Cricket Lui) provide additional detail.

Setting Up Your Network

There are many steps involved in preparing your network for an Internet connection, including:

- Getting an IP address and assigning unique addresses to each computer on your network.

- Getting a domain name, deciding on primary and secondary name servers to "advertise" your network to the rest of the Internet, and assigning host names to internal computers.

- Getting an In-Addr domain to map addresses into names.

- Preparing internal routing to utilize the Internet connection.

- Setting up Domain Name Service *(DNS)* software, minimally a resolver to get domain information for your users.

- Setting up mail transport—SMTP. Deciding between a centralized system or LAN distribution to individual workstations

- Gathering troubleshooting tools like ping and traceroute.

- Implementing security precautions.

- Setting up or distributing Internet application software to your users.

Some providers will assist, hands-on, in setting up your local configurations. Some providers will assist you by providing online or phone consulting help during your setup process. Many providers will provide both primary and secondary Domain Name Service for you, which will cut down the amount of work you need to do. Ask about what help is provided as part of the setup procedure.

Hardware and Software

The maintenance of the router at your site varies. This is a matter of personal preference. As previously discussed, it is easier for providers to update the routing, software, and hardware of a connection because they are familiar with the equipment. It is also much easier for them to troubleshoot the connection since they know what has been changed in the router at any time. Using the provider for maintenance is the only way you will get a service guarantee.

If you maintain your own router, the provider will have a more difficult time fixing your connection when it breaks. They will have to figure out everything you have changed in your router to get the big picture necessary to troubleshoot effectively. Placing your router in the hands of your provider's administrators may make your life a lot simpler and your Internet connection more robust.

It is important to define responsibility for maintenance of equipment. As much as possible, make sure that you know who is maintaining each piece of equipment in the connection, who is responsible for upgrades, who initiates troubleshooting in the event of a problem, and where the provider feels their general responsibilities lie.

Running an Internet connection can be handled by a knowledgable network administrator. There are plenty of training classes and books to teach them the ropes. Mailing lists on the Internet can be especially helpful. Good ones for Internet information are TCP/IP (tcp-ip-request@-nic.ddn.mil) and Big-Lan (big-lan-request@suvm.acs.syr.edu).

Routing Protocols

You may have a preference regarding the routing protocol used because of existing equipment that you are planning to use in your connection. Internet standard protocols include RIP and OSPF. There are other proprietary protocols that are implemented by router vendors and used by Internet providers. If you have a particular requirement like Cisco's IGRP, make sure your supplier can meet it.

User Support

Large organizations have large staffs who need training on uses of the Internet. Evaluate the user services department of the provider for the functions discussed in Chapter 4 if you need help training your staff. The User Services department should be able to provide resources to simplify training. The resources provided could be manuals, reference books, software packages, or recommendations, newsletters, and training classes.

Options

There are a number of services that are optional, but may be important to you. USENET News is easy to feed using a dedicated line connection, although it still is a disk hog. Check to see if the provider will give you a feed as part of the service. Be sure to identify if there is any additional charge.

Some sites don't want to bother with setting up a primary or secondary Domain Name Service. Check to see if you can get DNS from the provider and if there is an additional charge.

Multicast IP is the protocol which allows reception of Mbone feeds. If you have a 1.544 megabit-per-second connection or greater, this feature can be enabled. Check to see if these will be available through the provider and if there is any additional charge.

Backdoor Connections

Providers differ substantially when it comes to hooking up sites behind your connection. This type of connection is called a *backdoor connection*. Some providers let you hook up an entire corporate network. Some allow just local sites. Some allow connections to anybody. This is considered by most providers to be a reseller arrangement, even if you give your backdoor connections away for free. Some providers prohibit backdoor connections. If you think you may want the flexibility to add and delete backdoor connections, check into the provider's policy.

Remember that if you become a network provider by allowing backdoor connections through your network, the users will be asking the questions discussed in this book. There is the possiblity that your own internal network and your Internet connection will be affected adversely by additional traffic from backdoor connections. Be sure to evaluate the impact of backdoor connections throughly before offering them.

Installation

Most providers have a firm installation schedule that begins when an order is placed for an Internet connection and ends when the installation of the connection is completed and traffic can flow on the network. A host of tasks must be accomplished by both the provider and client to ensure that committed completion dates, also known as due dates, are met. Equipment and circuits must be ordered, configured, and installed. Software must be ordered and installed.

One provider's installation procedure starts with a site specification worksheet where the site is asked for various information such as technical and administrative contacts, IP addresses, domain names, the physical location where installation is to be performed, etc. When the provider receives this information, an installation date can be set based on the readiness of the site. It is not unusual for the provider to conduct a site survey to determine the optimal installation procedure. A reasonable installation date is 30 days after placing an order, which allows adequate time for the circuit to be installed by the telephone company.

Cost

Price structures vary considerably from provider to provider for dedicated line connections. Most provide flat rate services based on the speed of your link. Some are implementing usage-based pricing schemes, although these are new. Significant variations in costs are usually due to the equipment in the link and the maintenance and repair of the connection. You can own the equipment, you can rent it, or have a combination thereof. If you are an expert and feel that you can "do it yourself," you should consider a bare bones connection. In this case, you'd provide all of your own equipment and do your own maintenance and troubleshooting. If you are not an expert or you are an expert who wants a service guarantee, evaluate service levels from different providers. Costs are not always based on service levels. You can find really great connections for the same price as really poor ones.

Figure 6-2 provides a way to compare costs of dedicated line connections. When estimating costs, look at all the components it will take to get online. The chart was built for a standard connection as shown in Figure 6-1, but can be easily modified for use with other types of connections. For example, if you are choosing a frame relay connection, simply delete the columns that do not apply. The providers will be the best source for this information.

Dedicated Line Cost Comparison			
Service Provider	**1**	**2**	**3**
Connection Speed			
Installation Charge			
Monthly Network Charge			
Monthly Line Charge			
Local Router Cost			
Local CSU/DSU			
Port Connection Cost			
Remote CSU/DSU Cost			
Other Costs			
Total First Year Cost			
Total Near Future Costs			
Note:			
Service Provider	**4**	**5**	**6**
Connection Speed			
Installation Charge			
Monthly Network Charge			
Monthly Line Charge			
Local Router Cost			
Local CSU/DSU			
Port Connection Cost			
Remote CSU/DSU Cost			
Other Costs			
Total First Year Cost			
Total Near Future Costs			
Note:			
Comments:			

Figure 6-2. Typical dedicated line circuit speeds

Figure 6-3 shows an example comparing two providers using the comparison chart. In this example, a 56 kpbs connection was considered. A full service network, FastNet, was compared to a bare-bones network, HairNet, to comprehend the financial difference between the two. While the first year costs are about the same, since all the hardware has to be amortized, the second year costs differ substantially. It will be important to define precisely the extra service you will be receiving in order to justify the difference in price. In most cases, the extra expense will seem like a bargain in the long run if your network serves a large user community.

Dedicated Line Cost Comparison			
Service Provider	**1** FastNet	**2** HairNet	**3**
Connection Speed	56 kilobits/sec		
Installation Charge	1500	1500	
Monthly Network Charge	1250	800	
Monthly Line Charge	300	300	
Local Router Cost	included	4000	
Local CSU/DSU	included	650	
Port Connection Cost	included	0	
Remote CSU/DSU Cost	included	650	
Other Costs	none	none	
Total First Year Cost	21100	21000	
Total Near Future Costs	18600	13200	
Note:	Net Maintenance	Own Maintenance	
Service Provider **4**		**5**	**6**

Assumption: Equipment cost spread over first year.

Figure 6-3. Sample comparison of two providers

Contracts and Agreements

There will be an agreement or contract involved with a dedicated line connection which should be reviewed carefully. Look for language about service guarantees, installation schedules, equipment ownership, services provided, allowable data, cost, payment schedules, length of the agreement, and termination of the agreement. If an important issue is not spelled out in the agreement, ask for it to be included.

Dedicated Line Checklist of Questions

Circuits

What speed connection do I want?

Do I have a preferred method of attachment like SMDS or ATM?

Equipment Required

Do I have my own equipment that I want to use in the connection? Is it compatible with the suppliers?

Do I need a service guarantee?

Do I have the software necessary to set up my interconnectivity? Can I get it? Do I need help with setup? Will the provider help me?

Setting Up Your Network

Do I have an IP address? Can I get one from the provider?

Do I have a domain name? Will the provider assist me in getting one?

Am I planning to do name service locally? If not, will the provider find a primary and secondary name service for me? If so, will the provider find a secondary name service for me?

Do I have an In Addr domain? Will the provider assist me in getting one?

Have I set up my internal routing for interconnectivity? Will the provider assist me?

Have I figured out how I am going to deal with mail? If I am doing distributed mail delivery, does my software support SMTP? If I am doing centralized mail handling, do I have capacity to handle the users and mechanisms for account setup? Will the provider assist in setting up mail service?

Have I collected troubleshooting tools? Can I get them from the provider?

What is my security plan? What extra security features are offered by my provider?

Hardware and Software

Who maintains and repairs the router? The routing?

Who maintains and repairs the CSU/DSU? The circuit?

How does troubleshooting get initiated?

Do I have a preferred routing protocol? Does the supplier support it?

Do I need the support of a user service's department? Does the supplier have one?

Options

Do I want a USENET newsfeed? Can I get one? How much does it cost?

Do I want an Mbone feed? Can I get one? How much does it cost?

Am I planning to offer backdoor connections? Are there any restrictions on doing this from the provider? Am I really sure I want to do this?

Installation

Can the link be installed when I want it?

What is the installation schedule?

What are typical problems during installation?

Cost

How much does it cost?

What am I really getting for your money?

Contract

Have I reviewed the contract prior to issuing a purchase order?

Is everything okay with the terms and conditions?

The Public Dialup Internet Access List (PDIAL)

This appendix provides a list of public access service providers offering dialup access to outgoing Internet connections such as FTP and TELNET.

11 June 1993
Copyright 1992-1993 Peter Kaminski.
Reprinted with permission.
May be distributed but not sold—see the notice at the end of this document, or tell people to e-mail "Send PDIAL" to info-deli-server@netcom.com.

What Is PDIAL?

PDIAL is a list of Internet service providers offering public access dialup accounts and outgoing Internet access (FTP, TELNET, etc.). Most of them provide e-mail, USENET News and other services as well.

If one of these systems is not accessible to you and you need e-mail or USENET access but don't need FTP or TELNET, you have many more public access systems from which to choose. Public access systems without FTP or TELNET are not listed in this list, however. See the nixpub (alt.bbs, comp.misc) list and other BBS lists.

Some of these providers offer time-shared access to a shell or BBS program on a computer connected directly to the Internet, through which you can FTP or TELNET to other systems on the Internet. Usually other services are provided as well. Generally, you need only a modem and terminal or terminal emulator to access these systems. Check for "shell", "BBS", or "menu" on the services line.

Other providers connect you directly to the Internet via SLIP or PPP when you dial in. For these you need a computer system capable of running the software to interface with the Internet, e.g., a UNIX machine, PC, or Mac. Check for "SLIP" or "PPP" on the services line.

While I have included all sites for which I have complete information, this list is surely incomplete. Please send any additions or corrections to kaminski@netcom.com.

Providers with Wide Area Access

Table A-1. Providers of Public Data Network and 800-Accessible Connections

PDN	800
delphi	class
holonet	cns
michnet	crl
portal	csn
psi-gds	dial-n-cerf-usa
psilink	jvnc
well	OARnet
world	class

"PDN" means the provider is accessible through a public data network (check the listings below for which network); note that many PDNs listed offer access outside North America as well as within North America. Check with the provider or the PDN for more details.

"800" means the provider is accessible via a toll-free U.S. phone number. The phone company will not charge for the call, but the service provider will add a surcharge to cover the cost of the 800 service. This may be more expensive than other long-distance options.

Area Codes for US/Canada Dialup Accounts

If you are not Local to any of these providers, it's still likely you are able to access those providers available through a public data network (PDN). Check the section above for providers with wide area access.

Table A-2. Providers by Area Code

Area Code	Provider	Area Code	Provider
201	jvnc-tiger	513	OARnet
202	express, grebyn	514	CAM.ORG
203	jvnc-tiger	516	jvnc-tiger
206	eskimo, halcyon, netcom, nwnexus	517	michnet
212	mindvox, panix	603	MV, nearnet
213	dial-n-cerf, netcom	609	jvnc-tiger
214	metronet	614	OARnet
215	jvnc-tiger, PREPnet	616	michnet
216	OARnet, wariat	617	delphi, nearnet, world
301	express, grebyn	619	cyber, dial-n-cerf, netcom
303	cns, csn	703	express, grebyn
310	dial-n-cerf, netcom	704	rock-concert
312	genesis	707	crl
313	michnet, MSen	708	genesis
401	anomaly, ids, jvnc-tiger	713	sugar
408	a2i, netcom, portal	714	dial-n-cerf
410	express	717	PREPnet
412	PREPnet, telerama	718	mindvox, panix
415	crl, dial-n-cerf, netcom, portal, well	719	cns, csn, oldcolo
419	OARnet	814	PREPnet
503	agora.rain.com, netcom	815	genesis
508	anomaly, nearnet	818	dial-n-cerf, netcom
510	dial-n-cerf, holonet, netcom		

These are area codes Local to the dialups, although some prefixes in the area codes listed may not be Local to the dialups. Check your phone book or contact your phone company.

Most providers listed here are also accessible by packet-switched data services such as PC Pursuit ($30/month for 30 hours off-peak 2400 bps access—call 800-736-1130 for more information), traditional long distance services, and, of course, TELNET.

Phone Prefixes for International Dialup Accounts

If you are not Local to any of these providers, there is still a chance you are able to access those providers available through a public data network (PDN). Check the section above for providers with wide area access, and send e-mail to them to ask about availability.

+61 2 connect.com.au

+61 3 connect.com.au

+44 (0)81 Demon, ibmpcug

List of Providers

Fees are for personal dialup accounts with outgoing Internet access; most sites have other classes of service with other rate structures as well. Most support e-mail and netnews along with the listed services.

"Long distance: provided by user" means you need to use services such as PC Pursuit, direct dial long distance, or other long distance services.

a2i

Name	a2i communications
Dialup	408-293-9010 (v.32, v.32 bis) or 408-293-9020 (PEP) "guest"
Area code	408
Local access	CA: Campbell, Los Altos, Los Gatos, Moutain View, San Jose, Santa Clara, Saratoga, Sunnyvale
Long distance	Provided by user

Services	Shell (SunOS UNIX and MS-DOS), FTP, TELNET, feeds
Fees	$20/month or $45/3 months or $72/6 months
E-mail	info@rahul.net
Voice	408-293-8078 voice-mail
FTP more info	FTP.rahul.net:/pub/BLURB

agora.rain.com

Name	RainDrop Laboratories
Dialup	503-293-1772 (2400) 503-293-2059 (v.32, v.32 bis) "apply"
Area code	503
Local access	OR: Portland, Beaverton, Hillsboro, Forest Grove, Gresham, Tigard, Lake Oswego, Oregon City, Tualatin, Wilsonville
Long distance	Provided by user
Services	Shell, FTP, TELNET, Gopher, usenet
Fees	$6/month (1 hr/day limit)
E-mail	info@agora.rain.com
Voice	N/A
FTP more info	agora.rain.com:/pub/gopher-data/agora/agora

anomaly

Name	Anomaly—Rhode Island's Gateway To The Internet
Dialup	401-331-3706 (v.32) or 401-455-0347 (PEP)
Area code	401, 508
Local access	RI: Providence/Seekonk Zone
Long distance	Provided by user
Services	Shell, FTP, TELNET, SLIP
Fees	Commercial: $125/6 months or $200/year; Educational: $75/6 months or $125/year
E-mail	info@anomaly.sbs.risc.net
Voice	401-273-4669
FTP more info	anomaly.sbs.risc.net:/anomaly.info/access.zip

CAM.ORG

Name	Communications Accessibles Montreal
Dialup	514-281-5601 (v.32 bis, HST) 514-738-3664 (PEP), 514-923-2103 (ZyXeL 19.2K) 514-466-0592 (v.32)
Area code	514
Local access	QC: Montreal, Laval, South-Shore, West-Island
Long distance	Provided by user
Services	Shell, FTP, TELNET, feeds, SLIP, PPP, FAX gateway
Fees	$25/month Cdn.
E-mail	info@CAM.ORG
Voice	514-923-2102
FTP more info	N/A

clarknet

Name	Clark Internet Services, Inc. (ClarkNet)
Dialup	410-730-9786, 410-995-0271, 301-596-1626, 301-854-0446, 301-621-5216 'guest'
Area codes	202, 301, 410, 703
Local access	Baltimore MD, Washington DC, Northern VA
Long distance	Provided by user
Services	Shell, menu, FTP, TELNET, irc, Gopher, hytelnet, www, WAIS, SLIP/PPP, ftp space, feeds (UUCP & uMDSS), dns, Clarinet
Fees	$23 per month or $66 for 3 months or $126 for 6 months or $228 per year
E-mail	info@clark.net
Voice	Call 800-735-2258 then give 410-730-9764 (MD Relay Svc)
Fax	410-730-9765
FTP more info	ftp.clark.net:/pub/clarknet/fullinfo.txt

class

Name	Cooperative Library Agency for Systems and Services
Dialup	Contact for number; NOTE: CLASS serves libraries/information distributors only

Area code	800
Local access	Anywhere (800) service is available
Long distance	Included
Services	FTP, TELNET, Gopher, WAIS, hytelnet
Fees	$10.50/hour + $150/year for first account + $50/year each additional account + $135/year CLASS membership
E-mail	class@class.org
Voice	800-488-4559
Fax	408-453-5379
FTP more info	N/A

cns

Name	Community News Service
Dialup	719-520-1700 ID "new", passwd "newuser"
Area code	303, 719, 800
Local access	CO: Colorado Springs, Denver; continental US/800
Long distance	800 or provided by user
Services	UNIX shell, e-mail, FTP, TELNET, IRC, USENET, Clarinet, Gopher
Fees	$1/hour; $10/month minimum + $35 signup
E-mail	klaus@cscns.com
Voice	719-579-9120
FTP more info	N/A

connect.com.au

Name	connect.com.au pty ltd
Dialup	Contact for number
Area code	+61 3, +61 2
Local access	Australia: Melbourne, Sydney
Long distance	Provided by user
Services	SLIP, PPP, ISDN, UUCP, FTP, TELNET, NTP, FTPmail
Fees	AUS$2000/year (1 hour/day), 10% discount for AUUG members; other billing negotiable
E-mail	connect@connect.com.au

Voice	+61 3 5282239
Fax	+61 3 5285887
FTP more info	ftp.connect.com.au

crl

Name	CR Laboratories Dialup Internet Access
Dialup	415-389-UNIX
Area codes	415, 707, 800
Local access	CA: San Francisco Bay Area; continental US/800
Long distance	800 or provided by user
Services	Shell, FTP, TELNET, feeds, SLIP, WAIS
Fees	$19.50/month + $15.00 signup
E-mail	info@crl.com
Voice	415-381-2800
FTP more info	N/A

csn

Name	Colorado SuperNet, Inc.
Dialup	Contact for number
Area codes	303, 719, 800
Local access	CO: Alamosa, Boulder/Denver, Colorado Springs, Durango, Fort Collins, Frisco, Glenwood Springs/Aspen, Grand Junction, Greeley, Gunnison, Pueblo, Telluride; anywhere 800 service is available
Long distance	Provided by user or 800
Services	Shell or menu, UUCP, SLIP, 56K, ISDN, T1; FTP, TELNET, IRC, Gopher, WAIS, domains, anonymous FTP space, e-mail-to-fax
Fees	$1/hour off-peak, $3/hour peak ($250 max/month) + $20 signup, $5/hr surcharge for 800 use
E-mail	info@csn.org
Voice	303-273-3471
Fax	303-273-3475
FTP more info	csn.org:/CSN/reports/DialinInfo.txt
Off-peak	Midnight to 6 am

cyber

Name	The Cyberspace Station
Dialup	619-634-1376 "guest"
Area code	619
Local access	CA: San Diego
Long distance	Provided by user
Services	Shell, FTP, TELNET, IRC
Fees	$15/month + $10 startup or $60 for six months
E-mail	help@cyber.net
Voice	
FTP more info	N/A

Demon

Name	Demon Internet Systems (DIS)
Dialup	+44 (0)81 343 4848
Area code	+44 (0)81
Local access	London, England
Long distance	Provided by user
Services	FTP, TELNET, SLIP/PPP
Fees	GBPounds 10.00/month; 132.50/year (inc 12.50 startup charge). No on-line time charges.
E-mail	internet@demon.co.uk
Voice	+44 (0)81 349 0063
FTP more info	N/A

delphi

Name	DELPHI
Dialup	800-365-4636 "JOINDELPHI password:INTERNETSIG"
Area codes	617, PDN
Local access	MA: Boston; KS: Kansas City
Long distance	Sprintnet or Tymnet: $9/hour weekday business hours, no charge nights and weekends
Services	FTP, TELNET, feeds, user groups, wire services, member conferencing

Fees	$10/month for 4 hours or $20/month for 20 hours + $3/month for Internet services
E-mail	walthowe@delphi.com
Voice	800-544-4005
FTP more info	N/A

dial-n-cerf

Name	DIAL n' CERF or DIAL n' CERF AYC
Dialup	Contact for number
Area codes	213, 310, 415, 510, 619, 714, 818
Local access	CA: Los Angeles, Oakland, San Diego, Irvine, Pasadena, Palo Alto
Long distance	Provided by user
Services	Shell, menu, IRC, FTP, hytelnet, Gopher, WAIS, WWW, terminal service, SLIP
Fees	$5/hour ($3/hour on weekend) + $20/month + $50 startup OR $250/month flat for AYC
E-mail	help@cerf.net
Voice	800-876-2373 or 619-455-3900
FTP more info	nic.cerf.net:/cerfnet/dial-n-cerf/
Off-peak	Weekend: 5 pm Friday to 5 pm Sunday

dial-n-cerf-usa

Name	DIAL n' CERF USA
Dialup	Contact for number
Area code	800
Local access	Anywhere (800) service is available
Long distance	Included
Services	Shell, menu, IRC, FTP, hytelnet, Gopher, WAIS, WWW, terminal service, SLIP
Fees	$10/hour ($8/hour on weekend) + $20/month
E-mail	help@cerf.net
Voice	800-876-2373 or 619-455-3900
FTP more info	nic.cerf.net:/cerfnet/dial-n-cerf/
Off-peak	Weekend: 5pm Friday to 5pm Sunday

eskimo

Name	Eskimo North
Dialup	206-367-3837 300-2400 bps, 206-362-6731 for 9600/14.4k, 206-742-1150 World Blazer
Area code	206
Local access	WA: Seattle, Everett
Long distance	Provided by user
Services	Shell, FTP, TELNET
Fees	$10/month or $96/year
E-mail	nanook@eskimo.com
Voice	206-367-7457
FTP more info	N/A

express

Name	Express Access—Online Communications Service
Dialup	301-220-0462, 410-766-1855, 908-937-9481 "new"
Area codes	202, 301, 410, 703, 908
Local access	Northern VA, Baltimore MD, Washington DC, New Brunswick NJ
Long distance	Provided by user
Services	Shell, FTP, TELNET, IRC, Gopher, hytelnet, www
Fees	$25/month or $250/year
E-mail	info@digex.com
Voice	800-546-2010, 301-220-2020
FTP more info	N/A

genesis

Name	"genesis", MCSNet
Dialup	(312) 248-0900 V.32bis/V.32, 248-6295 (PEP), follow prompts
Area codes	312, 708, 815
Local access	IL: Chicago
Long distance	Provided by user
Services	Shell, FTP, TELNET, feeds, e-mail, IRC, Gopher

Fees	$25/month or $65/3 months
E-mail	info@genesis.mcs.com
Voice	N/A
FTP more info	N/A

grebyn

Name	Grebyn Corporation
Dialup	703-281-7997, "apply"
Area codes	202, 301, 703
Local access	Northern VA, Southern MD, Washington DC
Long distance	Provided by user
Services	Shell, FTP, TELNET
Fees	$30/month
E-mail	info@grebyn.com
Voice	703-281-2194
FTP more info	N/A

halcyon

Name	Halcyon
Dialup	206-382-6245 "new", 8N1
Area code	206
Local access	Seattle, WA
Long distance	Provided by user
Services	Shell, TELNET, FTP, BBS, IRC, Gopher, hytelnet
Fees	$200/year, or $60/quarter + $10 start-up
E-mail	info@halcyon.com
Voice	206-955-1050
FTP more info	halcyon.com:~/pub/waffle/info

holonet

Name	HoloNet
Dialup	510-704-1058
Area codes	510, PDN
Local access	Berkeley, CA

Long distance	[per hour, off-peak/peak] Bay Area: $0.50/$0.95; PSINet A: $0.95/$1.95; PSINet B: $2.50/$6.00; Tymnet: $3.75/$7.50
Services	FTP, TELNET, IRC, games
Fees	$2/hour off-peak, $4/hour peak; $6/month or $60/year minimum
E-mail	info@holonet.net
Voice	510-704-0160
FTP more info	holonet.net:/info/
Off-peak	5 pm to 8 am + weekends and holidays

ibmpcug

Name	UK PC User Group
Dialup	+44 (0)81 863 6646
Area code	+44 (0)81
Local access	London, England
Long distance	Provided by user
Services	FTP, TELNET, BBS, IRC, feeds
Fees	GBPounds 15.50/month or 160/year + 10 startup (no time charges)
E-mail	info@ibmpcug.co.uk
Voice	+44 (0)81 863 6646
FTP more info	N/A

ids

Name	The IDS World Network
Dialup	401-884-9002, 401-785-1067
Area code	401
Local access	East Greenwich, RI; northern RI
Long distance	Provided by user
Services	FTP, TELNET, SLIP, feeds, BBS
Fees	$10/month or $50/half year or $100/year
E-mail	sysadmin@ids.net
Voice	401-884-7856
FTP more info	ids.net:/ids.net

jvnc-tiger

Name	The John von Neumann Computer Network—Dialin' Tiger
Dialup	Contact for number
Area codes	201, 203, 215, 401, 516, 609, 908
Local access	Princeton & Newark, NJ; Philadelphia, PA; Garden City, NY; Bridgeport, New Haven, & Storrs, CT; Providence, RI
Long distance	Provided by user
Services	FTP, TELNET, SLIP, feeds, optional shell
Fees	$99/month + $99 startup (PC or Mac SLIP software included—shell is additional $21/month)
E-mail	info@jvnc.net
Voice	800-35-TIGER, 609-258-2400
FTP more info	N/A

jvnc

Name	The John von Neumann Computer Network—Tiger Mail & Dialin' Terminal
Dialup	Contact for number
Area code	800
Local access	Anywhere (800) service is available
Long distance	Included
Services	E-mail and newsfeed or terminal access only
Fees	$19/month + $10/hour + $36 startup (PC or Mac SLIP software included)
E-mail	info@jvnc.net
Voice	800-35-TIGER, 609-258-2400
FTP more info	N/A

metronet

Name	Texas Metronet
Dialup	214-705-2902 (9600bps), 214-705-2917 (2400bps), "info/info" or "signup/signup"
Area code	214

Local access	TX: Dallas
Long distance	Provided by user
Services	Shell, FTP, TELNET, feeds, SLIP
Fees	$10-$50/month + $20-$30 startup
E-mail	srl@metronet.com 73157.1323@compuserve.com GEnie:S.LINEBARG
Voice	214-401-2800
Fax	214-401-2802 (8 am-5 pm CST weekdays)
FTP more info	N/A

michnet

Name	Merit Network, Inc.—MichNet project
Dialup	Contact for number or TELNET hermes.merit.edu and type "help" at "Which host?" prompt
Area codes	313, 517, 616, 906, PDN
Local access	Michigan; Boston, MA; Wash. DC
Long distance	SprintNet, Autonet, Michigan Bell packet-switch network
Services	TELNET, SLIP, PPP, outbound SprintNet, Autonet and Ann Arbor dialout
Fees	$35/month + $40 signup ($10/month for K-12 & libraries in Michigan)
E-mail	info@merit.edu
Voice	313-764-9430
FTP more info	nic.merit.edu:/

mindvox

Name	MindVOX
Dialup	212-989-4141 "mindvox" "guest"
Area codes	212, 718
Local access	NY: New York City
Long distance	Provided by user
Services	Conferencing system FTP, TELNET, IRC, Gopher, hytelnet, Archives, BBS
Fees	$15-$20/month. No startup.

E-mail	info@phantom.com
Voice	212-989-2418
FTP more info	N/A

MSen

Name	MSen
Dialup	Contact for number
Area code	313
Local access	All of SE Michigan (313)
Long distance	Provided by user
Services	Shell, WAIS, Gopher, TELNET, FTP, SLIP, PPP, IRC, WWW, Picospan BBS, FTP space
Fees	$20/month; $20 startup
E-mail	info@msen.com
Voice	313-998-4562
Fax	313-998-4563
FTP more info	FTP.msen.com:/pub/vendor/msen

nearnet

Name	NEARnet
Dialup	Contact for numbers
Area codes	508, 603, 617
Local access	Boston, MA; Nashua, NH
Long distance	Provided by user
Services	SLIP, e-mail, feeds, dns
Fees	$250/month
E-mail	nearnet-join@nic.near.net
Voice	617-873-8730
FTP more info	nic.near.net:/docs

MV

Name	MV Communications, Inc.
Dialup	Contact for numbers
Area code	603

Local access	Many NH communities
Long distance	Provided by user
Services	Shell, FTP, TELNET, Gopher, SLIP, e-mail, feeds, dns, archives, etc.
Fees	$5.00/month minimum + variable hourly rates. See schedule.
E-mail	info@mv.com
Voice	603-429-2223
FTP more info	FTP.mv.com:/pub/mv

netcom

Name	Netcom Online Communication Services
Dialup	(206) 527-5992, (310) 842-8835, (408) 241-9760, (408) 459-9851, (415) 328-9940, (415) 985-5650, (503) 626-6833, (510) 426-6610, (510) 865-9004, (619) 234-0524, (916) 965-1371
Area codes	206, 213, 310, 408, 415, 503, 510, 619, 818, 916
Local access	CA: SF Bay Area (5 POPs), Sacramento, Santa Cruz, Los Angeles, San Diego; OR: Portland; WA: Seattle (May 1)
Long distance	Provided by user
Services	Shell, FTP, TELNET, IRC, WAIS, Gopher, SLIP/PPP, FTP space, feeds, dns
Fees	$19.50/month + $15.00 signup
E-mail	info@netcom.com
Voice	408-554-UNIX
FTP more info	N/A

nwnexus

Name	Northwest Nexus Inc.
Dialup	Contact for numbers
Area code	206
Local access	WA: Seattle
Long distance	Provided by user
Services	UUCP, SLIP, PPP, feeds, dns

Fees	$10/month for first 10 hours + $3/hr; $20 start-up
E-mail	info@nwnexus.wa.com
Voice	206-455-3505
FTP more info	nwnexus.wa.com:/NWNEXUS.info.txt

OARnet

Name	OARnet
Dialup	Send e-mail to nic@oar.net
Area codes	614, 513, 419, 216, 800
Local access	OH: Columbus, Cincinnati, Cleveland, Dayton
Long distance	800 service
Services	E-mail, FTP, TELNET, newsfeed
Fees	$4.00/hr to $330.00/month; call for code or send e-mail
E-mail	nic@oar.net
Voice	614-292-8100
Fax	614-292-7168
FTP more info	N/A

oldcolo

Name	Old Colorado City Communications
Dialup	719-632-4111 "newuser"
Area code	719
Local access	CO: Colorado Springs
Long distance	Provided by user
Services	Shell, FTP, TELNET, AKCS, home of the NAPLPS conference
Fees	$25/month
E-mail	dave@oldcolo.com / thefox@oldcolo.com
Voice	719-632-4848, 719-593-7575 or 719-636-2040
Fax	719-593-7521
FTP more info	N/A

panix

Name	PANIX Public Accss UNIX
Dialup	212-787-3100 "newuser"
Area codes	212, 718
Local access	New York City, NY
Long distance	Provided by user
Services	Shell, FTP, TELNET, Gopher, WAIS, IRC, feeds
Fees	$19/month or $208/year + $40 signup
E-mail	alexis@panix.com, jsb@panix.com
Voice	212-877-4854 [Alexis Rosen], 212-691-1526 [Jim Baumbach]
FTP more info	N/A

portal

Name	The Portal System
Dialup	408-973-8091 (high-speed), 408-725-0561 (2400bps); "info"
Area codes	408, 415, PDN
Local access	CA: Cupertino, Mountain View, San Jose
Long distance	SprintNet: $2.50/hour off-peak, $7-$10/hour peak; Tymnet: $2.50/hour off-peak, $13/hour peak
Services	Shell, FTP, TELNET, IRC, UUCP, feeds, BBS
Fees	$19.95/month + $19.95 signup
E-mail	cs@cup.portal.com, info@portal.com
Voice	408-973-9111
FTP more info	N/A
Off-peak	6pm to 7am + weekends and holidays

PREPnet

Name	PREPnet
Dialup	Contact for numbers
Area codes	215, 412, 717, 814
Local access	PA: Philadelphia, Pittsburgh, Harrisburg
Long distance	Provided by user

Services	SLIP, terminal service, TELNET, FTP
Fees	$1,000/year membership. Equipment-$325 onetime fee plus $40/month
E-mail	prepnet@cmu.edu
Voice	412-268-7870
Fax	412-268-7875
FTP more info	FTP.prepnet.com:/prepnet/general/

psi-gds

Name	PSI's Global Dialup Service (GDS)
Dialup	send e-mail to numbers-info@psi.com
Area code	PDN
Local access	
Long distance	included
Services	TELNET, rlogin
Fees	$39/month + $39 startup
E-mail	all-info@psi.com, gds-info@psi.com
Voice	703-620-6651
Fax	703-620-4586
FTP more info	FTP.psi.com:/

psilink

Name	PSILink—Personal Internet Access
Dialup	Send e-mail to numbers-info@psi.com
Area code	PDN
Local access	
Long distance	Included
Services	E-mail and newsfeed, FTP
Fees	$29/month + $19 startup (PSILink software included)
E-mail	all-info@psi.com, psilink-info@psi.com
Voice	703-620-6651
Fax	703-620-4586
FTP more info	FTP.psi.com:/

rock-concert

Name	Rock CONCERT Net
Dialup	Contact for number
Area codes	704, 919
Local access	NC: Asheville, Chapel Hill, Charlotte, Durham, Greensboro, Greenville, Raleigh, Winston-Salem, Research Triangle Park
Long distance	Provided by user
Services	Shell, FTP, TELNET, IRC, Gopher, WAIS, feeds, SLIP
Fees	$30/month + $50 signup
E-mail	info@concert.net
Voice	919-248-1999
FTP more info	FTP.concert.net

sugar

Name	NeoSoft's Sugar Land Unix
Dialup	713-684-5900
Area code	713
Local access	TX: Houston metro area
Long distance	Provided by user
Services	BBS, shell, FTP, TELNET, IRC, feeds, UUCP
Fees	$29.95/month
E-mail	info@NeoSoft.com
Voice	713-438-4964
FTP more info	N/A

telerama

Name	Telerama BBS
Dialup	412-481-5302 "new"
Area code	412
Local access	PA: Pittsburgh
Long distance	Provided by user
Services	Shell, FTP, TELNET, feeds, menu, BBS

Fees	$6/month for 10 hours, 60 cents/hour thereafter. No startup.
E-mail	info@telerama.pgh.pa.us
Voice	412-481-3505
FTP more info	telerama.pgh.pa.us:/info/general.info

well

Name	The Whole Earth 'Lectronic Link
Dialup	415-332-6106 "newuser"
Area codes	415, PDN
Local access	Sausalito, CA
Long distance	Compuserve Packet Network: $4/hour
Services	Shell, FTP, TELNET, BBS
Fees	$15.00/month + $2.00/hr
E-mail	info@well.sf.ca.us
Voice	415-332-4335
FTP more info	N/A

wariat

Name	APK- Public Access UNI* Site
Dialup	216-481-9436 (2400), 216-481-9425 (V.32bis, SuperPEP)
Area code	216
Local access	OH: Cleveland
Long distance	Provided by user
Services	Shell, FTP, TELNET, IRC, Gopher, feeds, BBS(Uni-board1.10)
Fees	$35/monthly, $200/6 months, $20 signup
E-mail	zbig@wariat.org
Voice	216-481-9428
FTP more info	N/A

world

Name	The World

Dialup	(617) 739-9753 'new'
Area codes	617, PDN
Local access	Boston, MA
Long distance	Compuserve Packet Network: $5.60/hour
Services	Shell, FTP, TELNET, IRC
Fees	$5.00/month + $2.00/hr or $20/month for 20 hours
E-mail	office@world.std.com
Voice	617-739-0202
FTP more info	world.std.com:/world-info/basic.info

How People Can Get the PDIAL List

USENET

The PDIAL list is posted semi-regularly to alt.internet.access.wanted, alt.bbs.lists, alt.online-service, ba.internet, and news.answers.

E-mail

From the Information Deli archive server (most up-to-date): To receive the current edition of the PDIAL, send e-mail with the subject "Send PDIAL" to info-deli-server@netcom.com. To subscribe to a list which receives future editions as they are published, send e-mail with the subject "Subscribe PDIAL" to "info-deli-server@netcom.com". To receive both the most recent and future editions, send both messages.

From the news.answers FAQ archive: Send e-mail with the message "send usenet/news.answers/pdial" to mail-server@rtfm.mit.edu. For help, send the message "help" to mail-server@rtfm.mit.edu.

FTP Archive Sites (PDIAL and Other Useful Information)

The Information Deli FTP site is: FTP.netcom.com:/pub/info-deli/public-access/pdial [192.100.81.100]

It can also be found at:

- VFL.Paramax.COM:/pub/pubnet/pdial [128.126.220.104] (used to be GVL.Unisys.COM)

- The Merit Network Information Center Internet information archive: nic.merit.edu:/internet/pdial [35.1.1.48]

- liberty.uc.wlu.edu:/pub/lawlib/internet.access [137.113.10.35]

- As part of the news.answers FAQ archive: rtfm.mit.edu:/pub/usenet/-news.answers/pdial [18.70.0.224]

Finding Public Data Network (PDN) Access Numbers

Here's how to get Local access numbers or information for the various PDNs. Generally, you can contact the site you're calling for help, too.

☞ Unless noted otherwise, set your modem to 7E1 (7 data bits, even parity, 1 stop bit) when dialing to look up access numbers by modem as instructed below.

BT Tymnet

For information and Local access numbers, call 800-937-2862 (voice) or 215-666-1770 (voice).

To look up access numbers by modem, dial a Local access number, hit <CR> and "a", and enter "information" at the "please log in:" prompt.

Compuserve Packet Network

You do *not* have to be a Compuserve member to use the CPN to dial other services.

For information and Local access numbers, call 800-848-8199 (voice).

To look up access numbers by modem, dial a Local access number, hit <CR> and enter "PHONES" at the "Host Name:" prompt.

PC Pursuit (SprintNet)

PC Pursuit may be used to call a modem in any of 44 major metro areas in the US from Local access numbers around the country. As such, it can be used to access most of the providers listed in the PDIAL (those with no other PDN access or even those which are accessible by other PDNs).

For information and registration, call 800-736-1130 (voice) or 800-877-2006 (data). More information is also available on the PC Pursuit support BBS (see below).

To look up access numbers by modem, dial 800-546-1000, hit <CR><CR><CR> at 1200 baud or "@"<CR><CR> at 2400 baud. Enter "MAIL" at the "@" prompt, then "PHONES" at the "USER NAME:" prompt, and "PHONES" at the "PASSWORD:" prompt.

The PC Pursuit support BBS provides a great deal of information about PC Pursuit, including rates, terms and conditions, outdial numbers, etc.

To access the PC Pursuit support BBS, dial a local access number and hit <CR><CR><CR> at 1200 baud or "@"<CR><CR> at 2400 baud. Change modem parameters to 8N1, and enter "C PURSUIT" at the "@" prompt.

PSINet

For information, call 800-82PSI82 (voice) or 703-620-6651 (voice), or send e-mail to all-info@psi.com. For a list of Local access numbers send e-mail to numbers-info@psi.com.

Copyright and Distribution of PDIAL; Other Notices

This document may be distributed in its entirety by any means, and a fee may be charged for its distribution, but it may not be sold without prior permission.

I make no representations about the suitability or accuracy of this document for any purpose. It is provided "as is" without express or implied warranty.

UPDATES AND CORRECTIONS: Send new or updated entries in the format used here to kaminski@netcom.com. Also include an e-mail address to which I can send requests for more information.

```
Peter Kaminski
kaminski@netcom.com (preferred)
The Information Deli
71053.2155@compuserve.com
connecting people"
```

In this chapter:
- *Alphabetic Provider Listing*
- *Database Service Providers*
- *Providers Based in Canada*
- *International Providers*
- *Alphabetic Provider Listing*

Internet Access Provider List

This appendix provides a printed copy of DLIST, an online list of Internet service providers who offer dedicated line connections. They may also offer dialup connections. The list is as complete as the author could make it on the date of publication. Any additions or corrections should be sent to update-dlist@ora.com. To find out how to receive an updated version of DLIST, send e-mail to dlist@ora.com.

The list is organized into five parts. First is an alphabetical listing of U.S. providers. Second is Database Service Providers. Third is a listing of providers in Canada. Fourth is a listing of providers outside of the U.S. and Canada. Fifth is a provider listing by state.

Alphabetic Provider Listing

AlterNet TCP/IP network service, UUNET Technologies, Inc.

Service Area:	US and International
Contact:	Alternet Sales
Voice:	800-4UUNET3, 703-204-8000
e-mail:	alternet-info@uunet.uu.net
FTP for more info	ftp.uu.net:~info/alternet

Network Description:
AlterNet provides Internet connectivity to organizations seeking access to the Internet. AlterNet connectivity options range from dialup SLIP/PPP up

to T1 and 10 mbps speeds. All traffic on AlterNet is unrestricted as UUNET Technologies owns and operates its own backbone service. The network is built from proven, off-the-shelf technology and AlterNet engineers enjoy close working relationships with those of the technology vendors.

ANS CO+RE Systems, Inc.

Service Area:	US and International
Contact:	Inside Sales
Voice:	800-456-8267 or 313-663-7610
e-mail:	info@ans.net
FTP more info:	ftp.ans.net (cd /pub)

Network Description:
ANS CO+RE Systems, Inc. is a provider of value-added network services for those businesses looking to solve their problems through the use of wide-area internetworking and the Internet. A wholly-owned subsidiary of Advanced Network & Services, Inc., ANS CO+RE Systems offers access to its T3 nationwide network and the Internet at a variety of connection speeds, from dialup to T3. ANS CO+RE also offers a complete suite of TCP/IP WAN services, including network connectivity, security services, systems integration, network engineering & design, implementation, operation, NOC outsourcing, training, and consulting. ANS CO+RE provides professional-quality services to all clients, connecting to over 10,000 different networks at a variety of interface points, thus offering robust interconnectivity.

BARRNet

Service Area:	Northern and Central California
Contact:	R. J. Goldberg
Voice:	415-723-7003 415-322-0602
e-mail:	info@barrnet.net
FTP more info:	ftp.barrnet.net

Network Description:
Organized in 1987, BARRNet is the NSFNET regional provider of Internet connectivity service to business, education and government in Northern and Central California. BARRNet offers premier high and low speed connectivity, as well as turn-key Internet installation and network consulting services.

BGnet

Service Area:	Bulgaria
Contact:	Daniel Kalchev
Voice:	+359-52-259135
Fax:	+359-52-234540
e-mail:	postmaster@Bulgaria.EU.net
FTP more info:	ftp.digsys.bg

Network Description:
BGnet provides Internet services to commercial, government, and academic users. Services include Electronic Mail (RFC-822 and X.400), Network News, Archive Access, and Internet Talk Radio using X.25, dialup (UUCP and IP), and leased line connectivity. BGnet is a member of EUnet and exchanges traffic with all major networks including the US regionals and NSFnet, and is a member of the Commercial Internet Exchange (CIX) and Ebone.

CENTnet, The Cambridge Entrepreneurial Network

Service Area:	Eastern Massachusetts
Contact:	Bill Love
Voice:	617-354-5800
e-mail:	love@ora.com
FTP more info:	N/A

Network Description:
CENTnet is a least-cost solution to dedicated and dialup Internetworking. Network service is at either 19.2k or 56k dedicated leased line or Dialup SLIP, (via one of our members—DMConnection.) CENTnet is a commercial Internet provider.

CERFnet

Service Area:	California and International
Contact:	Sales Manager
Voice:	800-8762373, 619-455-3900
e-mail:	help@cerf.net
FTP more info:	nic.cerf.net

Network Description:
CERFnet is a forward thinking Internet service provider for both the commercial and educational markets. CERFnet was one of the first

Internet service providers to address the growing needs of the commercial sector and is a founding member of the CIX (Commercial Internet Exchange). To meet the needs of the business community, CERFnet helped to develop new and innovative Internet services and was one of the first providers to offer dialup services via an 800 number, low cost hourly IP services, and advanced services such as SMDS. CERFnet also continues to support the academic community with programs such as the Global School House and CERF n' Safari. For the future, CERFnet is committed to providing quality Internet access and services at reasonable costs to all members of the user community.

CICNet

Coverage Area:	Minnesota, Wisconsin, Iowa, Indiana, Illinois, Michigan, Ohio
Contact:	Kimberly Shaffer
e-mail:	info@cic.net
Voice:	313-998-6104
FTP for more info	N/A

Network Description:

CICNet is a regional computer internetworking provider. A non-profit organization started by the schools of the Big Ten in 1988, CICNet provides connectivity to its Charter members, other higher education and K-12 organizations as well as commercial companies. At CICNet connectivity is more than a connection as is evident in the many seminars, tutorials, and user meetings this organization sponsors each year for its membership. With some of the nation's premier technical talent as a part of its membership, CICNet is a trend setter in the exploration of new technologies as well as providing a reliable high speed T-1 redundant network backbone for its customers.

CONCERT Network

Service Area:	North Carolina
Contact:	CONCERT-Connect
Voice:	919-248-1999
e-mail:	info@concert.net
FTP more info:	ftp.concert.net

Network Description:

CONCERT-CONNECT, a program of the MCNC Center for Communications, provides North Carolina businesses and industry an opportunity to access state and national research and education resources through the Internet. CONCERT, Communications for North Carolina Education, Research, and Technology, is a statewide IP data network currently operating a T1/T3 backbone connected to the Internet through a contract with Advanced Network and Services, Inc. CONCERT-CONNECT provides three types of connections: 1) Direct Connections, 56 Kbps or T1 circuit speeds, 2) Serial Line Internet Protocol (SLIP), dialup modem access for your local UNIX network, and 3) UUCP Mail/News, mail and/or news services only. Local network access is provided throughout the state with dialin access in the following North Carolina cities: Asheville, Chapel Hill, Charlotte,Durham, Greensboro, Greenville, Raleigh and Winston-Salem.

CSUnet

Service Area:	California
Contact:	Laura Guillory
Voice:	310-985-9641
e-mail:	laura@calstate.edu
FTP more info:	nic.csu.net or Gopher at eis.calstate.edu (vt100 login as csuinfo)

Network Description:
CSUnet is the largest network in the state of California, focused entirely on education. Comprised of 48 full members and more than 20 associate members, CSUnet spans the entire state of California with 35 T-1 circuits and 26 56K circuits. CSUnet has a point of presence in every one of California's 11 LATAs. Originally designed in 1984 to support the 19 (now 20) campuses of the California State University, CSUnet now includes all educational institutions throughout California in its mission, including K-12, Community Colleges, and public libraries. CSUnet is also a multiple-services network. In addition to data services, two-way compressed video between CSU campuses continues to grow at a rapid pace.

Global Enterprise Services, Inc.

Service Area:	US and International
Contact:	Marketing Department
e-mail:	market@jvnc.net
Voice:	800-35-TIGER
FTP more information:	N/A

Network Description:

Global Enterprise Services, Inc., through the John von Neumann Computer Network (JvNCnet), is a mature data communications network with seven years of experience in providing state-of-the-art Internet access and network services to commercial, academic, and government organizations in the United States and internationally. Formed in 1986, JvNCnet is one of the original networks comprising the National Science Foundation network (NSFNET), which in turn is an integral part of the Internet, and is a member of the Commercial Internet Exchange (CIX). GES provides high speed gateway and dialup connectivity to the Internet, as well as customized networking and training services.

ISI Network Associates

Service Area:	Los Angeles Area
Contact:	Joe Kemp
Voice:	310-822-1511
e-mail:	ina-info@isi.edu
FTP for more infa	in-notes/ina/isi-net-assoc-story on VENERA.ISI.EDU

Network Description:

The ISI Network Associates program is a high-quality, low-overhead service of the Information Sciences Institute of the University of Southern California to provide Internet access. There are currently 15 associate organizations in the program connected to ISI with dedicated 9.6 Kb, 56 Kb, and T1 lines. No dialup service is provided. This program is for small organizations that need dedicated Internet connections and can provide their own technical and user service.

Los Nettos

Service Area:	Los Angeles Area
Contact:	Joe Kemp
Voice:	310-822-1511
e-mail:	los-nettos-info@isi.edu
FTP for more infa	in-notes/los-nettos/los-nettos-story on VENERA.ISI.EDU

Network Description:

Los Nettos is a high-quality, low-overhead network in the Los Angeles area. There are currently nine sites interconnected with T1 lines. This is a network for large organizations that need dedicated high bandwidth

Internet connections and can provide their own technical and user service. No dialup service is available.

MichNet/Merit

Service Area:	Michigan
Contact:	Jeff Ogden
Voice:	313-764-9430
e-mail:	info@merit.edu
FTP more info:	nic.merit.edu

Network Description:
MichNet is the regional network operated by the Merit Network, Inc. MichNet is attached to NSFNET at 45 mbps and offers direct TCP/IP connections at 9.6K, 56K, and 1.5M bps as well as public dialin services from 23 Michigan cities and Washington, D.C. Merit also maintains gateways between the Internet and SprintNet and Autonet, two commercial X.25 networks. MichNet's focus is on education, research, and community service organizations, but connections are available to any organization in Michigan.

MIDnet

Service Area:	Arkansas, Iowa, Kansas, Missouri, Nebraska, Oklahoma, South Dakota
Contact:	MIDnet Information Center
Voice:	402-472-7600
e-mail:	nic@westie.mid.net
FTP more info:	westie.mid.net

Network Description:
MIDnet offers dedicated and dialup services to the seven state region of Arkansas, Iowa, Kansas, Missouri, Nebraska, Oklahoma, and South Dakota. MIDnet is one of the oldest regional networks, operating since the fall of 1987. In addition to the high speed reliable service, MIDnet members also received the benefits of volume discount contracts.

The Missouri Research and Education Network (MOREnet)

Service Area:	Missouri
Contact:	Bill Mitchell, Director

Voice: 314-882-2000

e-mail: BILL@MORE.NET

FTP more info: N/A

Network Description:

MOREnet—the Missouri Research and Education Network—is Missouri's "data highway" linking its member to one another and the Internet. Based on the TCP/IP suite of protocols, MOREnet provides remote login (TELNET), file transfer (FTP) services, electronic mail, and member support services. MOREnet currently has 39 members from higher education, K-12, public libraries, state and federal agencies, private corporations, and continues to grow rapidly. The primary mission of MOREnet is to provide collaborative networked information services to education in support of instruction, research, and public service. MOREnet is uniquely positioned to be a catalyst for providing network connectivity to all areas of the state in support of instruction, research, public service, and economic development.

MRNet

Service Area: Minnesota

Contact: Dennis Fazio

Voice: 612-342-2570

e-mail: Info@MR.Net

FTP more info: FTP.MR.Net

Gopher more info: Gopher.MR.Net

Network Description:

The Minnesota Regional Network (MRNet) is an independent nonprofit network service provider serving the state of Minnesota and nearby areas. It provides economical leased line access at 56Kb and T1 bandwidths via point-to-point link or Frame Relay (Twin Cities only). Educational and unrestricted commercial access is available. The MRNet dialIP Service is also available for lower-cost dialup SLIP access.

Msen

Service Area: Michigan, Ohio, Indiana, Illinois

Contact: Owen Medd

Voice: 313-998-4562

e-mail: info@msen.com

FTP more info: ftp.msen.com:/pub/vendor/msen

Network Description:
Msen provides a full range of Internet connection services to a wide array of organizations, both commercial and academic. From dialup access through high speed leased line services, Msen is able to tailor its services to fit the customer's needs. In addition, Msen can supply a growing number of custom information services, including a real-time Reuters news clipping service and a full-scale jobs and resumes database containing thousands of entries.

MV Communications, Inc. (mv.com)

Service Area:	New Hampshire and surrounding areas
Contact:	Mark Mallett or Marta Greenberg
Voice:	603-429-2223
e-mail:	info@mv.mv.com for autoreply, mv-admin@m-v.mv.com for human
FTP more info:	ftp.mv.com:/pub/mv

Network Description:
MV Communications provides many forms of Internet access for individuals, small businesses, and organizations. We offer UUCP access, interactive accounts, and SLIP/PPP connections. Our goal is to make the net affordable and within reach of everyone; we have discount programs for special organizations and educational use, and in general help to bridge that last mile between the network and the individual.

NEARnet

Service Area:	Maine, Vermont, New Hampshire, Connecticut, Rhode Island, Massachusetts, New York; additional areas served upon request.
Contact:	John Curran
Voice:	617-873-8730
e-mail:	nearnet-join@nic.near.net
FTP more info:	ftp.near.net

Network Description:
NEARnet is the premier Internet service for organizations in the New England region. NEARnet connects a wide range of universities, laboratories, and corporations with each other and millions of other users of the worldwide Internet. NEARnet supports access to research and educational organizations through the NSFNET and its affiliated regional networks. It also supports unequalled access to the commercial Internet via multiple

commercial networking services. NEARnet was founded by MIT, Harvard University, and Boston University and from 1989 to 1993 was operated under contract by Bolt, Beranek, and Newman (BBN). On July 1, 1993, NEARnet transitioned to a service offering of BBN Technology Services Inc. which is a wholly-owned subsidiary of Bolt, Beranek, and Newman, Inc.

NETCOM On-Line Communication Services, Inc.

Service Area:	Nationwide
Contact:	Ask for a Personal or Business Account Representative
Voice:	408-554-8649
e-mail:	info@netcom.com
FTP for info:	N/A

Network Description:
NETCOM has a nationwide network connecting local points of presence in the following cities: Seattle, Portland, Sacramento, San Francisco, Berkeley, Pleasanton, Palo Alto, San Jose, Santa Cruz, Los Angeles, Santa Ana, San Diego, Dallas, Houston, Austin, Atlanta, Wash. DC, Boston, Chicago, Detroit, Denver. These points of presence allow local access with no connect time charges. NETCOM is a full service Internet connection provider.

netILLINOIS

Service Area:	Illinois
Contact:	Peter Roll, Executive Director or Joel L. Hartman, President
Voice:	708-467-7655 or 309-677-3100
e-mail:	p-roll@nwu.edu or joel@.bradley.edu
FTP more info:	N/A

Network Description:
netILLINOIS provides direct connections to the Internet at 56 Kb/s and T1 speeds, currently through backbone network nodes in four Illinois cities. Dial access service is beginning to be offered in the Chicago area. netILLINOIS does not at this time provide host computer services such as UUCP, e-mail, and newsgroup feeds or TELNET and FTP, although e-mail POP accounts and a limited selection of newsgroups are available to dial-access SLIP subscribers.

NevadaNet

Service Area:	Nevada
Contact:	Maurice Mitchell
Voice:	702-895-4580
e-mail:	mitch@nevada.edu
FTP more info:	N/A

Network Description:

NevadaNet is an initiative of the University and Community College System of Nevada with funding assistance from the National Science Foundation and the State of Nevada. NevadaNet is a state-wide network and currently serves the University of Nevada, Reno, including the University of Nevada School of Medicine; University of Nevada, Las Vegas; Desert Research Institute in Reno and Las Vegas; Community College of Southern Nevada in North Las Vegas; Northern Nevada Community College in Elko; Truckee Meadows Community College in Reno; and Western Nevada Community College in Carson City. A hub in Reno is connected to the Network Operation Center in Las Vegas via two T1 (1.54 mbps) circuits. The Las Vegas NOC is connected to the NSFNET backbone in San Diego via a T1 circuit. NevadaNet is a TCP/IP network with connections available up to T1. NevadaNet also provides compressed video connections between its units through the use of multi-point control units.

NorthWestNet

Service Area:	Pacific Northwest including AK, ID, MT, ND, OR, and WA
Contact:	NorthWestNet NIC
Voice:	206-562-3000
e-mail:	nic@nwnet.net
FTP more info:	ftp.nwnet.net

Network Description:

NorthWestNet is a regional (mid-level) network providing digital communication links based upon the Internet Protocol (IP) suite to NSFNET, Commercial Internet Exchange (CIX), and the Internet for knowledge-based organizations in the Pacific Northwest. Members include universities, colleges, higher education networks, K-12 schools and school districts, research labs, libraries, health care sites, state government agencies, industrial research centers, and businesses. NorthWestNet's mission is to promote research, education, and economic development by providing access to network communications, computing and electronic information systems and services throughout the Northwest. Some of NorthWestNet's services include Internet documentation and training; technical, user, and information services; working groups; annual meetings; "The Internet Passport"; and the NodeNews newsletter.

NYSERNet

Service Area:	New York
Contact:	Member Services
Voice:	315-453-2912
e-mail:	info@nysernet.org
Gopher more info:	telnet nysernet.org, login: nysernet (all lowercase)

Network Description:
NYSERNet is a high speed data network that connects New York State to the Internet. At this writing, NYSERNet's affiliate base includes just under two hundred organizations, from large research centers and universities, to small public libraries and K-12 schools. NYSERNet, Inc., is a not-for-profit 501(c)(3) corporation.

OARnet

Service Area:	Ohio and surrounding states
Contact:	Demetris Socli, Manager of Client Services
Voice:	614-292-8100
e-mail:	demetris@oar.net
FTP more info:	ftp.oar.net or use gopher.oar.net

Network Description:
OARnet offers dialup, leased line, and ISDN connections to the Internet. Clients dial a local number in Ohio cities, a "950" number elsewhere in Ohio, and an 800 number for areas outside Ohio. Leased line connections may be made to hubs in Cincinnati, Akron, Dayton, Columbus, Toledo, and Cleveland. We also offer internet-related services such as gopher installation, posting client material on the OARnet gopher, consulting on DNS, SMTP mail setup, and IP routing. OARnet also offers the ANS Interlock Security Service which provides comprehensive protection including encryption and support for key card authentication.

PI-net (Prospect Innovation Network)

Service Area:	Prospect Hill Office Park, Waltham, MA
Contact:	James A. Warner, Jr., Director
Voice:	617-890-6960
e-mail:	jwarner@prospect.com
FTP more info:	N/A

Network Description:

PI-net is a fiberoptic-based backbone network which connects the companies in the buildings of the Prospect Hill office park to the Internet through three 10 mbps microwave links of NEARnet, the New England regional network. Prospect Hill is a first class office park which is home to a large concentration of software and other technology companies from Interleaf and Microsoft to creative startups. PI-net provides the highest bandwidth connections on the Internet for prices below the lowest bandwidth typical dedicated services as a service to Prospect Hill companies only.

Public Access Networks Corp. (Panix Public Access Internet)

Service Area:	Metro New York City, Long Island, NJ, more in 1994.
Contact:	Alexis Rosen
Voice:	212-877-4854
e-mail:	alexis@panix.com
FTP more info:	gopher to gopher.panix.com or finger info@-panix.com.

Network Description:

We started out as a provider of dialup internet access. We have expanded dramatically in 1993 and we are now making dedicated lines available. Our first customer installation is scheduled for early August, 1993.

PREPnet

Coverage area:	Pennsylvania
Contact:	Thomas Bajzek
Voice:	412-268-7870
e-mail:	nic@prep.net
FTP more info:	nic.prep.net

Network Description:
PREPnet has been operating since 1988 as a regional network serving Pennsylvania. PREPnet has over 120 members from the higher education, business and industry, government agency, health care, K-12, library, and non-profit sectors. Service is available by connections to hubs in Pittsburgh, Harrisburg, Philadelphia, Allentown, Scranton, State College, and Meadville, which are linked by a T1 backbone. Dialin service is available in Pittsburgh, Harrisburg, Philadelphia, and Scranton. Access to the NSFNET is via a gateway at the Pittsburgh Supercomputing Center. Commercial use is available via ANS CO+RE to members who pay a surcharge for this service.

PSINet

Service Area:	US and International
Contact:	Inside Sales
Voice:	800-82psi82 (800-827-7482) or 703-620-6651
e-mail:	info@psi.com
FTP for more infa	ftp.psi.com, cd ~uuc

Network Description:
PSINet is a US-based commercial TCP/IP and Frame Relay full spectrum internetwork. It is currently a T1 backbone network with a T3-based ATM (Asynchronous Transfer Mode) system being deployed in 1993. PSI offers a variety of internetworking services providing corporate and individual users access to the Internet. Services range from leased-line to dialup access, as well as wireless e-mail.

RAINet

Service Area:	Northern Oregon & Southern Washington
Contact:	Randy Bush
Voice:	503-297-8820
e-mail:	admin@rain.com
FTP more info:	ftp.psg.com

Network Description:
RAINet was formed 1n 1990 to provide minimal-cost networking to the general public in the Portland/Vancouver area, not excluding the classic R&E and commercial users. RAINet currently has over 30 sites, and supports both dedicated line users and dialup SLIP/PPP users as well as a large number of UUCP sityes strung off the IP backbone. Costs are abso-

lutely minimal, with much of the operational labor being done in exchange for connectivity.

SDSCnet

Service Area: San Diego

Contact: Tom Perrine

Voice: 619-534-8328

e-mail: tep@sdsc.edu

Network Description:

The San Diego Supercomputer Center provides high speed network connections to support research activities, university systems, and a few local sites in the San Diego area. We have connections to NSFnet, CSUnet, UNvnet, UCOPnet and expect to have connection to the new vBNS, NCEnet and a local ATM-based MAN.

SESQUINET

Service Area: Texas, Mexico

Contact: Farrell Gerbode

Voice: 713-527-6038

e-mail: info@sesqui.net

FTP more info: ftp.sesqui.net:/pub/sesquinet/*

Network Description:

SESQUINET provides TCP/IP service service using multi-protocol routers from hubs in Houston, Dallas, Austin, and San Antonio which are interconnected by 1544Kb/s DS-1 circuits. A subscriber site is connected typically by a 56Kb/s or 1544Kb/s digital leased line connecting an network router at the subscriber site to a network router at a hub site. In the typical configuration, SESQUINET acquires and installs the leased line, the leased line CSU or CSU/DSU equipment and the network router at the subscriber site. A lower cost 9.6Kb/s dedicated LAN dialup service is offered in the Houston and Dallas local calling areas. Subscribers pay an initial connection fee, an annual fee based on the speed of the network connection and the actual cost of the communication lines to a hub site.

SprintLink

Coverage Area: US

Contact: Bob Doyle

Voice: 703-904-2167

e-mail: bdoyle@icm1.icp.net

FTP more info: N/A

Network Description:
SprintLink is a public data network service providing switched data network transport based on the Transmission Control Protocol/Internet Protocol (TCP/IP). SprintLink service is designed for users requiring Wide Area Network (WAN) connectivity for LAN-to-LAN networking and/or users requiring internetwork capability. SprintLink service is available from all 30+ Sprint Points of Presence (POPS) and is installed using dedicated access circuits between the customer premise and the Sprint POP. Access speeds for the service range from 9.6 DDS to 1.54 mbps. In addition to access to the SprintLink network, SprintLink customers can also access (via SprintLink) the Commercial Internet Exchange (CIX) and the Internet. SprintLink is also available using Integrated T1 Access Partitioning. Specifically, Sprint customers are able to integrate SprintLink service on T1 Access circuits that may also be used for other Sprint services.

STARnet

Service Area: Missouri (St. Louis metropolitan area)

Contact: Chris Myers

Voice: 314-935-7390

e-mail: chris@wugate.wustl.edu

FTP more info: NA

Network Description:
STARnet provides low-cost, fixed-rate access to the Internet via UUCP, dialup SLIP/PPP connections, and 56K or T1 leased-line access.

SURAnet

Service Area: West Virginia, Virginia, South Carolina, North
                     Carolina, Tennessee, Kentucky, Louisiana, Mississippi, Alabama, Georgia, Florida, Washington
                     DC, Maryland, Delaware, Puerto Rico, and South
                     America

Contact: Marketing Department

Voice: 301-982-4600

e-mail: marketing@sura.net

FTP more info: ftp.sura.net

Network Description:

SURAnet is a regional wide-area network serving the southeastern United States, Puerto Rico and South America. Our backbone comprises a robust mesh of dedicated lines connected to routers which are collocated in a major carrier's Points of Presence (POPs). SURAnet currently has 17 POPs within its region, with future plans to expand the coverage of its backbone and take advantage of new technologies to serve its members.

SwipNet

email: info@swip.net

Network Description:

SWIPnet (Swedish IP NETwork) is the first and largest public commercial IP operator in Sweden, established 1991 as an initiative of SNUS (Swedish Network Users Association) and the Swedish Unix Users Association. SwipNet is a subsidary of Tele2, the second new telephone company in Sweden. Gateways to Internet through NORDUNET, Ebone, GIX, etc. Current Internet **services include**: direct TCP/IP router connection up to 2 mbps; SLIP/CSLIP service up to 14.4 kbps; UUCP service up to 14.4 kbps; TELNET dial up service up to 14.4 kbps; X400/RFC 822 mail conversion facility.

Telerama

Service Area: Pittsburgh, PA

Contact: Kristen McQuillin

Voice: 412-481-3505

e-mail: info@telerama.pgh.pa.us

FTP more info: telerama.pgh.pa.us:/info/general-info

Network Description:

Telerama is dedicated to low-cost full Internet connectivity. We have a dedicated TCP/IP link and dialin pool and provide e-mail, Netnews (with UPI/Clarinet), Telnet, FTP, IRC, FSP, and UNIX access at a single low monthly rate. You can dial data direct for more information and to set up an account at 412-481-5302. We will be offering a dedicated line service in October 1993.

THEnet

Service Area: Texas

Contact: THEnet Network Information Center

Voice: 512-471-2400

e-mail: info@nic.the.net

FTP more info: N/A

Network Description:
THEnet provides Internet access only for organizations which work in direct support of research or education in Texas, or which hold state or federal government contracts. We do not sell to the general public. THEnet provides Internet access for state and federal government agencies. The research/education/governmental restriction does not preclude THEnet from having commercial members. We have many commercial members on THEnet, but they meet the research/education/governmental requirements.

UANet

Service Area: University of Arizona

Contact: Larry Rapagnani

Voice: 602-621-6666

e-mail: rapagnani@arizona.edu

FTP more info: N/A

Network Description:
Network for University of Arizona.

Washington Education Network (WEdNet)

Service Area: Washington State

Contact: Jill Hanson

Voice: 206-775-8471 ext. 4500

e-mail: jhanson@wsipc.wednet.edu

FTP more info: N/A

Network Description:
The Washington Education Network (WEdNet) is a statewide private digital network for educational institutions. WEdNet is capable of carrying data, voice, and interactive video teleconferencing simultaneously. It is administered by the Washington School Information Processing Cooperative (WSIPC) to meet the telecommunications needs of member educational entities within the State of Washington. The network T1 backbone connects WSIPC, nine Educational Service Districts, and the Office of the Superintendent for Public Instruction (OSPI). To achieve connectivity, schools have three options: dialup, multiplexed, or routed

connections between their network and the WEdNet via 56 kb or T1 leased lines depending upon their needs. Several data centers are hosting timeshare Internet systems for districts not ready for routed connections. Current membership includes 276 school districts, 9 ESD's, OSPI, and the Communications Technology Center (CTC), a computing consortium representing Washington Community & Technical Colleges.

Westnet

Service Area:	Arizona, Colorado, southern Idaho, New Mexico, Utah, Wyoming
Contact:	Pat Burns
Voice:	303-491-7260
e-mail:	pburns@westnet.net
FTP more info:	anonymous to westnet.net

Network Description:
Westnet is a collaborative effort among the five and one-half state region. It is managed by a Steering Committee comprised of individuals from the five and one-half states. Westnet is a collaborative effort between Colorado State University (which manages the effort) and the University of Colorado at Boulder (which provides technical support).

WiscNet

Service Area:	Wisconsin
Contact:	Jess Anderson
Voice:	608-262-5888
e-mail:	wn-info@nic.wiscnet.net
FTP more info:	nic.wiscnet.net

Network Description:
WiscNet provides connectivity for its members, which comprise higher education, government, and associated research and business enterprises within the State of Wisconsin.

World dot Net

Service Area:	Oregon, Washington, Idaho, Utah
Contact:	Internetworks, Inc. Sales
Voice:	206-576-7147
e-mail:	info@world.net

FTP more info: ftp.world.net:/pub/world.net

Network Description:
Internetworks, Inc. operates its high speed global internet connectivity service "World dot Net" over a private data network constructed in early '92. This network provides access to the internet at speeds up to 10 mbps as well as dedicated transmission facilities tailored for supporting private internetworks.

WVNET

Service Area:	West Virginia
Contact:	Harper Grimm
Voice:	304-293-5192
e-mail:	cc011041@wvnvms.wvnet.edu
FTP more info:	N/A

Network Description:
WVNET is a West Virginia state agency whose primary purpose is to provide computing and networking support to West Virginia public higher education.

Database Service Providers

AT&T InterNIC Directory and Database Services

Contact:	Erik Grimmelmann or Subu Subramanian
Voice:	800-862-0677 or 908-668-6587
e-mail:	admin@ds.internic.net

Service Description: InterNIC Directory and Database Services serves as your pointer to numerous resources on the network and offers the following services. The DIRECTORY OF DIRECTORIES provides even novice users references to information resources on the Internet and support a variety of access methods and tools. InterNIC DIRECTORY SERVICES provides you with white and yellow pages type services allowing for easy access and communication with other people and organizations, as well as providing you with large volumes of information at your fingertips. InterNIC DATABASE SERVICES provides you access to a wide variety of databases, documents, and other information. These services also supplement and make available the numerous resources that the education community and various affinity groups have and can share with the Internet community. AT&T invites users, organizations, companies, and other resource providers to participate in the effort by providing information in the DIRECTORY OF DIRECTORIES, DIRECTORY SERVICES or DATABASE SERVICES.

Msen, Inc.

Contact: Owen Medd
Voice: 313-998-4562
e-mail: info@msen.com

Service Description: The Msen Archive Service offers a wide range of methods to put data on the net for both free and for-pay consumption. Using a customer-selected combination of presentation methods, Msen allows you to make your data widely visible using methods such as FTP, Gopher, and WAIS.

Providers Based in Canada

ARnet

Service Area: Alberta
Contact: Walter Neilson
Voice: 403-450-5187
e-mail: neilson@TITAN.arc.ab.ca

BCnet

Service Area: British Columbia
Contact: Mike Patterson
Voice: 604-822-3932
e-mail: Mike@BC.net
FTP more info: ftp.BC.net

Network Description:
BCnet specializes in LAN-to-LAN interconnect using the TCP/IP protocol family providing access to the world-wide Internet. It originally focused on education, research and development, and technology transfer, and now carries unrestricted traffic. Its clients include all of the province's universities, the majority of its community colleges, and research labs and research-oriented companies, schools, libraries, hospitals, and governmental organizations.

fONOROLA

Service Area:	Canada
Contact:	Hung Vu
Voice:	613-235-3666
e-mail:	hungv@fonorola.net
FTP more info:	ftp.fonorola.net (directory /pub)

Network Description:

fONOROLA provides the first cross Canada commercial internet services in a wide range of access arrangements to customers in Toronto, Montreal, Ottawa, Vancouver with plans to expand these services to Calgary, Halifax and Quebec City. fONOROLA's backbone network is attached to ANS's T3 backbone at three locations across the continent.

MBnet

Service Area:	Manitoba
Contact:	Gerry Miller
Phone:	204-474-8230
e-mail:	miller@ccm.UManitoba.ca

*NB*net*

Service Area:	New Brunswick
Contact:	David MacNeil
Phone:	506-453-4573
e-mail:	DGM@unb.ca

NLnet

Service Area:	Newfoundland and Labrador
Contact:	Wilf Bussey
Phone:	709-737-8329
e-mail:	wilf@kean.ucs.mun.ca

NSTN

Service Area:	Nova Scotia
Contact:	Michael Martineau
Voice:	902-468-NSTN
e-mail:	martinea@hawk.nstn.ns.ca

FTP more info: N/A

Network Description:
Need to communicate effectively with a remote site? Interested in consulting with experts around the globe? Want an inexpensive way to access a commercial service such as Dialog? Don't waste resources establishing your communication network! NSTN Inc. has the expertise to design and manage a network completely suited to your needs. Your personal resources and location do not limit NSTN Inc.'s ability to link you to the world. They offer many personal connectivity solutions. NSTN Inc. services the internal communication requirements of organizations of all sizes. NSTN Inc.'s infrastructure brings your colleagues, workstations, regional offices, and associate companies together electronically.

ONet

Service Area:	Ontario
contact:	John Drake
Voice:	416-525-9140 x4000; AFTER OCT 15 '93: 905-525-9140 x24000
e-mail:	drake@mcmaster.ca
FTP more info:	onet.on.ca

Network Description:
Network limited to use for education, research and development, and technology transfer by both public and private sector members.

PEINet

Service Area:	Prince Edward Island
Contact:	Scott Fletcher or Jim Hancock
Voice:	902-566-0552
e-mail:	fletcher@upei.ca or hancock@upei.ca
FTP for more info	atlas.upei.ca

Network Description:
PEInet is an emerging regional network currently operating out of the University of PEI. In the fall of 1993, PEInet will begin commercial operation, offering full connection, SLIP, and host-based dialup network services.

RISQ

Service Area:	Quebec
Contact:	Bernard Turcotte
Voice:	514-340-5700
e-mail:	turcotte@crim.ca

SASKnet

Service Area:	Saskatchewan
Contact:	Dean C. Jones
Voice:	306-966-4860
e-mail:	jonesdc@admin.usask.ca

International Providers

AARNet

Service Area:	Australia
Contact:	AARNet Support
Voice:	+61-6-249-3385
e-mail:	aarnet@aarnet.edu.au
FTP for more info	Anonymous ftp on jatz.aarnet.edu.au in the directory '/pub/doc'.

Network Description:
AARNet is the Australian Academic and Research Network. The charter of AARNet is to provide computer-based communications services to the Australian academic and research community.

CARNet

Service Area:	Croatia
Contact:	Predrag Pale
Voice:	+38-41-629-963
e-mail:	Predrag.Pale@carnet.hr
FTP:	carnet.hr
Gopher:	carnet.hr

Network Description:
CARNet (Croatian Academic and Research Network) is an IP, leased-line national network. It will allow access to any non-profit organization or anybody for non-profit activities. It supports e-mail, TELNET and FTP as well as multiple Gopher servers. It also provides public dialup access.

Center for Science Networks in GMD

Service Area:	Germany
Contact:	Klaus Birkenbihl
Voice:	+49-2241-14-3177
e-mail:	Klaus.Birkenbihl@gmd.de
FTP more info:	N/A

Network Description:
The Center for Science networks provides connectivity, technical support (including planning and engineering) and network management and operations for communication service providers and large corporate networks.

CESNET

Service Area:	Czech Republic
Contact:	Dr.Jan Gruntorad
Voice:	+42-2-3117532
e-mail:	tkjg@earn.cvut.cz
FTP more info:	gopher.vslib.cz (147.230.16.1)

Network Description:
CESNET—Czech Educational and Scientific Network—connects Universities, research institutes, and other organizations located in Prague, Liberec, Plzen, Ceske Budejovice, Pardubice, Hradec, Kralove, Brno, Olomouc, Ostrava, Opava and Karvina. Typical line speeds—64 (19.2) kbps, cca 40 CISCO routers installed.

Chinese Research Network (CRN)

Contact:	Xiaofan Zhao
Voice:	+86-1-201-7661 x646
E-mail:	xiaofan.zhao@crn.cn

Network Description:
The Chinese Research Network (CRN), founded in 1987, aims at providing electronic communication means, based on the PSDN and any

available communication networks, to the Chinese scientsts, engineers, professors, and other researchers to facilitate them in exchanging information and coordinating cooperation with their partners in China and abroad. Eight members of CRN have been interconnected at present, including research institutes, universities, and academic organizations in Beijing, Shanghai, Chengdu, and Shijiazhuang. More institutions will join CRN in the future.

CNS (Chernikeeff Networking Services)

Service Area:	UK
Contact:	Ian Harding
Voice:	+44-932-814-800
e-mail:	cns@chernikeeff.co.uk
FTP more info:	NA

Network Description:
CNS is a new, UK-based commercial internetworking service, offering quality full Internet and/or Virtual Private Network connectivity to organizations. The service is scheduled to go live second half 1993. International partners of CNS are ANS CO+RE Systems Inc.

Demon Internet Ltd

Service Area:	United Kingdom
Contact:	Grahame Davies or Cliff Stanford
Voice:	+44-81-349-0063
e-mail:	internet@demon.net
FTP more info:	ftp.demon.co.uk /pub/doc/*.txt

Network Description:
We provide full Internet dialup connectivity starting from UKP 10 per month for a single host to UKP 100 for a Class C network. We also offer leased line access from UKP 250 per month. We have currently in excess of 1,500 Internet customers.

DKnet

Service Area:	Denmark
Contact:	DKnet
Voice:	+45-39-17-99-00
e-mail:	netpasser@dknet.dk

FTP more info: ftp.dknet.dk:/dknet—some information in Danish

Network Description:

Danish provider of EUnet services. Provides anything ranging from personal login accounts to leased line IP connections.

EUnet

Service Area: Europe, Northern Africa, and the former Soviet Union region.

Voice: +31 20 592 5109

e-mail: info@eu.net

Mail contact: In nearly every country in the EUnet operating region, send mail to: postmaster@<country>.eu.net. For general information (or for multi-country requests) write to postmaster@eu.net.

FTP for more info   ftp.eu.net:pub/info

Network Description:

EUnet provides AUP-free networking and Internet services to commercial, government, and academic users. Services include electronic mail (RFC-822 and X.400), network news, archive access, and Internet Talk Radio over ISDN, X.25, dialup (UUCP and IP), and leased line connectivity. EUnet's own infrastructure ranges from Washington DC to Vladivostok in Eastern Russia, enabling EUnet's 26 national service providers to bring a unique mix of international connectivity and local service to the user. EUnet exchanges traffic with all major networks including the US regionals and NSFnet, and is a member of the Commercial Internet Exchange (CIX) and Ebone.

EUnet Austria

Service Area: Austria

Contact: EUnet support

Voice: +43-1-3174969

e-mail: office@eunet.co.at

FTP more info: eunet.co.at:~ftp/pub/EUnet/EUnet-Austria

Network Description:

EUnet Austria is part of EUnet system and provides Internet connectivity and Frame Relay service through a wide range of access options. EUnet Austria is open to any institution interested in open networking without limitations on traffic types. Access is possible via the EUnet Point-of-Presence network (active POPs in Vienna, Linz, Graz and Salzburg, with four more POPs planned for 1994) through leased lines, Dialup IP and UUCP mail and news service via modems, ISDN, and the public X.25 network Datex-P.

EUnet Belgium

Service Area:	Belgium
Contact:	EUnet Belgium, p/a K.U.Leuven, Dept. Computer Science
Voice:	+32 16 201015 x3561
e-mail:	postmaster@Belgium.EU.net

EUnet Czechia

Service Area:	The Czech Republic
Contact:	Pavel Rosendorf
Voice:	+42-2-332-3242
e-mail:	prf@Czechia.eu.net
FTP more info:	ftp.EUnet.cz

Network Description:

EUnet Czechia is the Czech part of the EUnet network. EUnet Czechia offers network services from the low end (e-mail services over the uucp protocol) up to the full connectivity to the Internet using the full suite of TCP/IP protocols. Eunet Czechia has currently three POPs (Points-of-Presence) in major cities of the Czech Republic (Prague, Pilsen, Brno).

EUnet Deutschland

Service Area:	Germany
Voice:	+49-231-972-00
e-mail:	info@Germany.EU.net
FTP more info:	ftp.Germany.EU.net

Network Description:

EUnet Deutschland is the German part of EUnet, in operation since 1984 and offering Internet connectivity in a wide range of solutions. EUnet Deutschland is open to any institution interested in open networking without limitations on traffic types. Access is possible via Points-of-Presence in Dortmund, Hamburg, Kiel, Berlin Aachen, Frankfurt and Munich, via the public X25 network Datex-P, ISDN, dedicated leased lines, and dialup connections.

EUnet Finland

Service Area:	Finland
Contact:	Johan Helsingius
Voice:	+358-0-400-2060
e-mail:	helpdesk@EUnet.fi
FTP more info:	info.eunet.fi:/EUnet

Network Description:
EUnet Finland is the Finnish part of the pan-European EUnet network. Services include electronic mail (RFC-822 and X.400), network news, file transfer, remote login, archive access, mailbox service and directory services. Both UUCP and IP protocols are supported.

EUnet-Goya

Service Area:	Spain
Contact:	Juan A. Esteban (PR) or Inmaculada Pindado (Technical) or Francisca Jimenez (Administration)
Voice:	+34-1-413-4856
e-mail:	request@eunet.es
FTP more info:	goya.eunet.es:info/doc/EUnet/help, login anonymous

Network Description:
Goya Servicios Telematicos provides EUnet services in Spain, including e-mail, network news, Internet access, and customized business solutions. Oriented to a wide range of commercial customers, Goya provides national and international connectivity to hundreds of companies and institutions, from private research departments to financial companies. Access facilities include public X25, dialup, and leased lines.

EUnet Portugal

Service Area:	Portuguese Republic
Contact:	Jose Legatheaux Martins
Voice:	+351-1-295 44 64
e-mail:	pr@puug.pt
FTP more info:	ftp.puug.pt

Network Description:
EUnet Portugal provides EUnet services in the Portuguese Republic (e-mail, news, IP connectivity very soon).

EUnet Slovakia

Service Area:	Slovak Republic
Contact:	Gejza Buechler / Ivan Lescak
Voice:	+42-7-377-434 / +42-7-725-306
e-mail:	bb-op@Slovakia.EU.net
FTP more info:	ftp.eunet.sk

Network Description:
EUnet Slovakia provides EUnet services in Slovak Republic; these services include e-mail, news, Internet connectivity, and some additional services. Access to the services is possible via telephone network, public data network or leased line. There are no restrictions on customer profile nor AUP on a commercial basis.

EUnet Switzerland

Service Area:	Switzerland, Lichtenstein
Contact:	Simon Poole
Voice:	+41-1-291-45-80
e-mail:	info@eunet.ch
FTP more info:	ftp.eunet.ch, directory eunet

Network Description:
EUnet provides a wide range of professional and commercial networking services in Switzerland and Lichtenstein. Besides UUCP and X.400 based Mail and News, direct Internet access via dialup, X.25, ISDN, and leased lines is provided. Installation and consulting services are available on request. EUnet Switzerland is a AUP free network. EUnet Switzerland currently has local access points in Zuerich, Basel, Geneva, and Lugano and connects via EUnet's European infrastructure to other networks

Fnet (EUnet—France)

Service Area:	France
Contact:	Laurent Bloch & Veronique Dubillot
Voice:	+33-1-45-21-02-04 (Paris area)
e-mail:	contact@fnet.fr

FTP more info: ~ftp/Fnet on indus.fnet.fr

Network Description:

Fnet is the French branch of pan-European EUnet network. It provides access to the Internet through a variety of communication media (leased lines, public X.25, ISDN, and dialup phone) and provides mail, usenet news, and network support services. Services are also available for the individual or mobile user.

GARR

Service Area: Italy

Contact: GARR-NIS (GARR Network Information Service)

Voice: +39 -50-593360

e-mail: info@nis.garr.it

FTP more info: ftp.nis.garr.it:/garr

Network Description:

GARR is the acronym for Harmonisation Group for Research Networks created in 1988 operating under the Ministry of the University and of Scientific and Technological Research (MURST) in Italy. GARR is also the name of the Italian Research Network. The aim of GARR is to establish and operate a backbone interconnecting the Italian research and academic networks and to coordinate connections to international networks. The GARR network has been constituted to serve primarily the users of all institutions reporting to MURST and other public funded research institutions. The network services are also accessible by research departments of private initiatives which have cooperations and common projects with public funded research environment.

HEAnet (Higher Education Authority Network)

Service Area: Ireland

Contact: Mike Norris

Voice: +353-1-6612748

Fax: +353-1-6610492

e-mail: mnorris@hea.ie

Network Description:

HEAnet is the Irish academic and research network. It provides IP and other protocol services to A&R institutions in Ireland, and IP access to the Internet.

HEPNET-J

Contact:	Yukio Karita
Voice:	+81-298-64-1092
e-mail:	karita@kek.jp
FTP more info:	N/A

Network Description:

HEPNET-J locates Cisco routers in more than 20 universities in Japan and has a 192kbps terrestrial line connected from KEK to the ESnet's Cisco router located in NASA-Ames in US. Main protocols used in HEPNET-J are DECnet and TCP/IP.

INFNet

Service Area:	Italy
Contact:	Vistoli, Cristina
Voice:	+39-51-498260
e-mail:	cnaf@infn.it
FTP more info:	nic.infn.it/infnet-doc

Network Description:

INFNet is the nationwide network of the Italian National Institute for Nuclear Physics (INFN), founded to provide the access to existing national and international HEP Laboratories, national Computing Center and to facilitate the communication between the researchers.

Internet Initiative Japan

Service Area:	Japan
Contact:	Kimiko Ishikawa (Japanese), Toshiya Asaba (English)
Voice:	+81-3-3580-3781
e-mail:	info@iij.ad.jp
FTP more info:	ftp.iij.ad.jp:/pub/info/English for English language versions or /pub/info/Japanese for Japanese language versions

Network Description:

Internet Initiative Japan offers both anonymous and subscriber UUCP services and will be offering full Appropriate Use Policy-free IP services starting September 1993 with connection speeds ranging from 9.6 kbps to 1.5 mbps or higher. Connectivity to the Internet outside of Japan is provided via a 768 kbps dedicated line to the US. Initially, IIJ will be providing local access facilities in the Kanto region, later expanding to Kansai, Kyushu, Hokkaido, and other regions of Japan.

ISnet

Service Area:	Iceland
Contact:	Marius Olafsson
Voice:	+354-1-694747
e-mail:	isnet-info@isgate.is
FTP more info:	N/A

Network Description:
ISnet provides Internet connectivity to all interested organizations in Iceland, via its connections to NORDUnet and EUnet.

IUnet

Service Area:	Italy
Contact:	Alessandro Berni
Voice:	+39-10-3532747
FTP more info:	ftp.iunet.it

Network Description:
IUnet is the Italian part of EUnet, in operation since 1986 and offering Internet connectivity in a wide range of solutions. IUnet is open to any institution interested in open networking without limitations on traffic types. Access is possible via the IUnet Point-of-Presence network (active POPs in Genoa, Milan, Rome, and Turin; new POPs are planned by the end of the year), via the public X25 network ITAPAC and via dialup connections.

NLnet

Service Area:	The Netherlands
Contact:	O.M. Roos Lindgreen / Ted Lindgreen
Voice:	+31-20-592-4245
e-mail:	info@NL.net
FTP more info:	ftp.NL.net:gopher/NLnet

Network Description:

NLnet provides Internet services in the Netherlands, either based on TCP/IP or on UUCP. Connections are made via leased lines or dialup phone lines. NLnet is the Dutch part of EUnet.

Pipex

Service Area:	United Kingdom
Contact:	Richard Nuttall (technical) and Mark Hugo (sales)
Voice:	44-223-250120
e-mail:	sales@pipex.net
FTP more info:	ftp.pipex.net

Network Description:

PIPEX Limited (part of the Unipalm group) introduced commercial Internet connectivity to the UK in 1992, and now has well over a hundred leased line customers, with many more accessing via dialup. In connecting them to a worldwide Internet comprised of over 15,000 networks and tens of millions of users, PIPEX relieves commercial users of such problems as line brokerage, hardware utilization and network redundancy, making connectivity more economical by virtue of the scale on which it operates, and its ability to negotiate interconnectivity agreements with other networks. PIPEX is a full member of CIX (Commercial Internet Exchange), alongside the world's other major IP network providers.

RCCN

Service Area:	Portugal
Contact:	Graca Carvalho
Voice:	+351-53-604475
e-mail:	ip-adm@rccn.net
FTP more info:	info.rccn.net

Network Description:

The RCCN (Rede da Comunidade Cientifica Nacional), is the Portuguese Research and Education Network funded by the FCCN (Fundacao de Calculo Cientifico Nacional)—the Foundation for the Development of National Scientific Computing. It is a research oriented network open to membership to any research institution or company, either public or private. No restrictions on membership apply provided that joining institutions abide by its acceptable use policy: RCCN backbone and common application services are provided to support open research and education among Portuguese research and educational institutions, plus research departments of companies when engaged in open communication for collaborative research. Use for other purposes, such as for-profit activities and extensive private or personal business is not acceptable.

SINET (Science Information NETwork)

Contact:	Prof. Shoichiro Asano
Voice:	+81-3-3942-2351
e-mail:	asano@nacsis.ac.jp
FTP more info:	N/A

Network Description:
SINET is an infrastructual Japanese IP backbone funded by Ministry of Education, Science and Culture for support communication for researchers at research institutes. SINET is composed of nine NOC currently. Domestically, 128-256 kbps circuits are installed between NOCs and soon be upgraded to 512 kbps. More than 50 universities are to be connected to NOCs using any routers. NACSIS is also providing JIX (Japan Internet eXchange) service where HEPNET-J, BITNET-J, and WIDE are already connected and ISASnet will be connected shortly. SINET and NACSIS have a 192 kbps circuit to FIX-W at NASA-Ames in US.

SURFnet

Service Area:	The Netherlands
Contact:	SURFnet HelpDesk
Voice:	+31-30-310290
e-mail:	info@surfnet.nl
FTP more info:	Host: ftp.nic.surfnet.nl [192.87.46.3], Dir: surfnet

Network Description:
The Dutch computer network SURFnet has been set up for staff and students in research and higher education in the Netherlands. There are 140 connected organizations. As a national network SURFnet interconnects the local networks of the affiliated institutes. In addition, SURFnet provides links with other domestic and international networks, both research networks (such as Internet, EARN/CREN, Europanet and EUnet) and public networks. SURFnet supports two protocols: X.25 and IP.

SWITCH

Service Area:	Switzerland
Contact:	SWITCH Head Office, Limmatquai 138, CH-8001 Zurich
Voice:	+41-1-268-15-15
e-mail:	hostmaster@switch.ch or C=CH;ADMD=ArCom;-PRMD=SWITCH;O=SWITCH;S=hostmaster;
FTP more info:	nic.switch.ch:/network

Network Description:
SWITCH is a foundation, sponsored by the government and the Swiss universities, providing teleinformatics services to all Swiss universities and to various research institutes by connecting to national and international resources. SWITCHlan is a national backbone network which connects all universities using leased lines with speeds between 128 kbps and 2 mbps. Most other organizations are connected via 64 kbps. The protocols supported are DECnet, TCP/IP, X.25, and ISO CLNS.

System Development Network(SDN)/HANA

Contact:	Dr. Jooyoung Song
Voice:	+82-2-526-5077
e-mail:	jysong@ring.kotel.co.kr
FTP more info:	NA

Network Description:
SDN/HANA is operated by member organizations. SDN/HANA has two committees, one is administrative and the other is technical. SDN/HANA is being managed at Korea Telecom Research Center and has 14 domestic sites. Korean(KSC5601, the national standard codeset) is supported in e-mail system as well as ASCII using encoding scheme based on ISO2022. SDN is connected to the Internet with 56 kbps satellite leased line between KAIST, Taejun and FIX-West, NASA-Ames, USA. It will be changed 192 kbps terrestrial line in the near future.

TANet, The Taiwan Academic Network

Contact:	Computer Center, Ministry of Education
Phone:	+886-2-7377439
E-mail:	nisc@twnmoe10.edu.tw or nisc@twnmoe10.bitnet
FTP more info:	ftp.edu.tw or moers2.edu.tw

Network Description:

TANet, The Taiwan Academic Network, is a pilot project undertaken by the Ministry of Education and Universities Computer Center to establish a common national academic network infrastructure. To support research and academic institutions in Taiwan, TANet will provide access to unique resources and opportunities for collaborative work. TANet will be the major part of the Taiwan Internet community which includes other industry network such as SEEDNet. A international link bandwidth was migrated from 64 kbps to 256 kbps between the Ministry of Education Computer Center and Princeton University (JvNCnet) in November 1992. This link couples TANet with JvNCnet, NFSnet, and international Internet connection. University/institutions may apply for membership.

TIPnet

Service Area:	Sweden
Contact:	Telia (sales), Unisource Business Networks (technical)
Voice:	90-400 (Telia), 08-688-20-00 (Unisource Business Networks)
e-mail:	info@tip.net (English: info-eng@tip.net)
FTP more info:	N/A

Network Description:

TIPnet is the Internet access network provided by Telia (Telia was previously known as Televerket—The Swedish Telecom). The service TIP (Telia IP service) is operated and developed by Unisource Business Networks in Sweden. TIP is available at the access rates 9.6, 19.2 and 64 kbps. The network has international connectivity via Ebone, Alternet, and Datanet using high speed Frame Relay links. TIP is the Swedish gateway to The World!

Provider Listing by State

Alabama
  Alternet
  ANS
  Global Enterprise Services
  Netcom
  PSINet
  SprintLink
  SURAnet

Alaska
  Alternet
  ANS
  Global Enterprise Services
  Netcom
  NorthwestNet
  PSINet
  SprintLink

Arizona
  Alternet
  ANS
  Global Enterprise Services
  Netcom
  PSINet
  SprintLink
  Westnet

Arkansas
  Alternet
  ANS
  Global Enterprise Services
  MIDnet
  Netcom
  PSINet
  SprintLink

California
  Alternet
  ANS
  BARRNet (Northern and Central)
  CERFnet
  Global Enterprise Services
  ISI Network Associates (Los
  Angeles)
  Los Nettos (Los Angeles)
  Netcom
  PSINet
  SDSCnet (San Diego)
  SprintLink

Colorado
  Alternet
  ANS
  Colorado Supernet
  Global Enterprise Services
  Netcom
  PSINet
  SprintLink
  Westnet

Connecticut
  Alternet
  ANS
  Global Enterprise Services
  NEARnet
  Netcom
  PSINet
  SprintLink

Delaware
  Alternet
  ANS
  Global Enterprise Services
  Netcom
  PSINet
  SprintLink
  SURAnet

Florida
  Alternet
  ANS
  Global Enterprise Services
  Netcom
  PSINet
  SprintLink
  SURAnet

Georgia
  Alternet
  ANS
  Global Enterprise Services
  Netcom
  PSINet
  SprintLink
  SURAnet

Hawaii
   Alternet
   ANS
   Global Enterprise Services
   Netcom
   PACCOM
   PSINet
   SprintLink

Idaho
   Alternet
   ANS
   Global Enterprise Services
   Netcom
   NorthwestNet
   PSINet
   SprintLink
   Westnet (Southern)
   World dot Net

Illinois
   Alternet
   ANS
   CICNet
   Global Enterprise Services
   Netcom
   netIllinois
   PSINet
   SprintLink

Indiana
   Alternet
   ANS
   CICNet
   Global Enterprise Services
   INet
   Netcom
   PSINet
   SprintLink

Iowa
   Alternet
   ANS
   CICNet
   Global Enterprise Services
   MIDnet
   Netcom
   PSINet
   SprintLink

Kansas
   Alternet
   ANS
   Global Enterprise Services
   MIDnet
   Netcom
   PSINet
   SprintLink

Kentucky
   Alternet
   ANS
   Global Enterprise Services
   Netcom
   PSINet
   SprintLink
   SURAnet

Louisiana
   Alternet
   ANS
   Global Enterprise Services
   Netcom
   PSINet
   SprintLink
   SURAnet

Maine
   Alternet
   ANS
   Global Enterprise Services
   NEARnet
   Netcom
   PSINet
   SprintLink

Maryland
   Alternet
   ANS
   Global Enterprise Services
   Netcom
   PSINet
   SprintLink
   SURAnet

Massachusetts
   Alternet
   ANS
   Global Enterprise Services
   NEARnet
   Netcom
   PSINet
   SprintLink

Michigan
   Alternet
   ANS
   CICNet
   Global Enterprise Services
   MichNet/Merit
   MSEN
   Netcom
   PSINet
   SprintLink

Minnesota
   Alternet
   ANS
   CICNet
   Global Enterprise Services
   MRNet
   Netcom
   PSINet
   SprintLink

Mississippi
   Alternet
   ANS
   Global Enterprise Services
   Netcom
   PSINet
   SprintLink
   SURAnet

Missouri
   Alternet
   ANS
   Global Enterprise Services
   MIDnet
   Netcom
   PSINet
   SprintLink

Montana
   Alternet
   ANS
   Global Enterprise Services
   NorthwestNet
   Netcom
   PSINet
   SprintLink

Nebraska
   Alternet
   ANS
   Global Enterprise Services
   MIDnet
   Netcom
   PSINet
   SprintLink

Nevada
   Alternet
   ANS
   Global Enterprise Services
   Netcom
   NevadaNet
   PSINet
   SprintLink

New Hampshire
   Alternet
   ANS
   Global Enterprise Services
   NEARnet
   Netcom
   PSINet
   SprintLink

New Jersey
   Alternet
   ANS
   Global Enterprise Services
   Netcom
   PSINet
   SprintLink

New Mexico
   Alternet
   ANS
   Global Enterprise Services
   Netcom
   PSINet
   SprintLink
   Westnet

New York
   Alternet
   ANS
   Global Enterprise Services
   NEARnet
   Netcom
   NYSERNet
   Panix
   PSINet
   SprintLink

North Carolina
  Alternet
  ANS
  CONCERT-CONNECT
  Global Enterprise Services
  Netcom
  PSINet
  SprintLink
  SURAnet

North Dakota
  Alternet
  ANS
  Global Enterprise Services
  Netcom
  NorthwestNet
  PSINet
  SprintLink

Ohio
  Alternet
  ANS
  CICNet
  Global Enterprise Services
  Netcom
  OARnet
  PSINet
  SprintLink

Oklahoma
  Alternet
  ANS
  Global Enterprise Services
  MIDnet
  Netcom
  PSINet
  SprintLink

Oregon
  Alternet
  ANS
  Global Enterprise Services
  Netcom
  NorthwestNet
  PSINet
  RAINet
  SprintLink
  World dot Net

Pennsylvania
  Alternet
  ANS
  Global Enterprise Services
  Netcom
  PREPnet
  PSINet
  SprintLink
  Telerama

Rhode Island
  Alternet
  ANS
  Global Enterprise Services
  NEARnet
  Netcom
  PSINet
  SprintLink

South Carolina
  Alternet
  ANS
  Global Enterprise Services
  Netcom
  PSINet
  SprintLink
  SURAnet

South Dakota
  Alternet
  ANS
  Global Enterprise Services
  MIDnet
  Netcom
  PSINet
  SprintLink

Tennessee
  Alternet
  ANS
  Global Enterprise Services
  Netcom
  PSINet
  SprintLink
  SURAnet

Texas
    Alternet
    ANS
    Global Enterprise Services
    Netcom
    PSINet
    Sesquinet
    SprintLink
    THEnet

Utah
    Alternet
    ANS
    Global Enterprise Services
    Netcom
    PSINet
    SprintLink
    Westnet

Vermont
    Alternet
    ANS
    Global Enterprise Services
    NEARnet
    Netcom
    PSINet
    SprintLink

Virginia
    Alternet
    ANS
    Global Enterprise Services
    Netcom
    PSINet
    SprintLink
    SURAnet
    VERnet

Washington
    Alternet
    ANS
    Global Enterprise Services
    Netcom
    NorthwestNet
    PSINet
    RAINet
    SprintLink
    World dot Net

Washington, D.C.
    Alternet
    ANS
    Global Enterprise Services
    Netcom
    PSINet
    SprintLink
    SURAnet

West Virginia
    Alternet
    ANS
    Global Enterprise Services
    Netcom
    PSINet
    SprintLink
    SURAnet
    WVNET

Wisconsin
    Alternet
    ANS
    CICNet
    Global Enterprise Services
    Netcom
    PSINet
    SprintLink
    WISCNet

Wyoming
    Alternet
    ANS
    Global Enterprise Services
    Netcom
    NorthwestNet
    PSINet
    SprintLink
    Westnet

Glossary

56K	A 64 kbps circuit with 8 kbps used for signalling. Sometimes called DDS or ADN.
64K	A 64 kbps circuit (DSO). "Clear Channel" is 64 kbps where entire bandwidth is used.
AUP	Acceptable Use Policy; the collective term used to refer to the restrictions placed on use of a network; usually refers to restrictions on use for commercial purposes.
application	(a) Software that performs a particular useful function for you. ("Do you have an electronic mail application installed on your computer?"); (b) The useful function itself (e.g., transferring files is a useful application of the Internet.)
Archie	A system for locating files that are publicly available by anonymous FTP.
ARPAnet	An experimental network established in the 1970's where the theories and software on which the Internet is based were tested. No longer in existence.
backbone	A major high-speed access point to which other networks are connected.
baud	When transmitting data, the number of times the medium's "state" changes per second. For example: a 2400 baud modem changes the signal it sends on the phone line 2400 times per second. Since each

change in state can correspond to multiple bits of data, the actual bit rate of data transfer may exceed the baud rate. Also, see bits-per-second.

BIND The UNIX implementation of DNS (q.v.). It stands for "Berkeley Internet Name Domain."

bits-per-second (bps)

The speed at which bits are transmitted over a communications medium.

byte A set of 8 bits; kilobytes (thousand bytes), megabytes (million bytes), and gigabytes (trillion bytes) indicate the size of data; in Internet standards-monger's lingo, an "octet."

CIX Commercial Internet Exchange; an agreement among network providers that allows them to exchange commercial traffic. Although it has been discussed a lot in the press, it's primarily a concern for network providers.

client A software application (q.v.) that works on your behalf to extract some service from a server somewhere on the network. Think of your telephone as a client and the telephone company as a server to get the idea.

CSU/DSU Channel Service Unit/Digital Service unit. Connects to the Telco company "channel" (56K/64K or T1) and provides a V.35 or RS232 connection to your network equipment (such as a router).

DDN Defense Data Network; a portion of the Internet which connects to U.S. Military Bases and contractors; used for non-secure communications. MILNET is one of the DDN networks. It also runs "the NIC," where a lot of Internet information is archived.

dedicated line A permanently connected private telephone line between two locations. Leased lines are typically used to connect a moderate-sized local network to an Internet service provider.

dialup line (a) A method of connecting to a computer by calling it up on the telephone. Often, "dialup" refers only to the kind of connection you make when using a terminal emulator and a regular modem. For the tech-

	noids: switched character-oriented asynchronous communication. (b) A port (q.v.) that accepts dialup connections.
DNS	The Domain Name System; a distributed database system for translating computer names (like *ruby.or-a.com*) into numeric Internet addresses (like *194.56.78.2*), and vice-versa. DNS allows you to use the Internet without remembering long lists of numbers.
DoD	The (U.S.) Department of Defense, whose Advanced Research Projects Agency got the Internet started by creating the ARPAnet.
DS0	Digital Signal Level 0 (64 kbps).
DS1	Digital Signal Level 1 (T1).
Ethernet	A kind of "local area network." It's pretty confusing because there are several different kinds of wiring, which support different communication speeds, ranging from 2 to 10 million bits-per-second. What makes an Ethernet an Ethernet is the way the computers on the network decide whose turn it is to talk. Computers using TCP/IP are frequently connected to the Internet over an Ethernet.
FAQ	Either a frequently asked question, or a list of frequently asked questions and their answers. Many USENET news groups, and some non-USENET mailing lists, maintain FAQ lists (FAQs) so that partici-pants won't spend lots of time answering the same set of questions.
flame	A virulent and (often) largely personal attack against the author of a USENET posting. "Flames" are unfor-tunately common. People who frequently write flames are known as "flamers."
Freenet	An organization to provide free Internet access to people in a certain area, usually through public libraries.
FT1	Fractional T1; a "fraction" of a T1 that uses less than 24 DS0s.

FTP	(a) The File Transfer Protocol; a protocol that defines how to transfer files from one computer to another. (b) An application program which moves files using the File Transfer Protocol. FTP is described in detail in Chapter 6, *Moving Files: FTP.*
gateway	A computer system that transfers data between normally incompatible applications or networks. It reformats the data so that it is acceptable for the new network (or application) before passing it on. A gateway may connect two dissimilar networks, like DECnet and the Internet; or it might allow two incompatible applications to communicate over the same network (like mail systems with different message formats). The term is often used inter-changeably with "router" (q.v.), but this usage is incorrect.
Gopher	A menu-based system for exploring Internet resources.
IAB	The Internet Architecture Board; the "ruling council" that makes decisions about standards and other important issues.
IETF	The Internet Engineering Task Force; a volunteer group that investigates and solves technical problems, and makes recommendations to the IAB (q.v.).
Internet	(a) Generally (not capitalized), any collection of distinct networks working together as one. (b) Specifically (capitalized), the world-wide "network of networks" that are connected to each other, using the IP protocol and other similar protocols. The Internet provides file transfer, remote login, electronic mail, news, and other services.
IP	The Internet Protocol; the most important of the protocols on which the Internet is based. It allows a packet to traverse multiple networks on the way to its final destination.
IRC	Internet Relay Chat; an Internet-based application that allows users to interact in real-time.

ISDN	Integrated Services Digital Network; a new kind of dialup connection offering higher speed access over voice lines.
ISO	The International Organization for Standardization; an organization that has defined a different set of network protocols, called the ISO/OSI protocols. In theory, the ISO/OSI protocols will eventually replace the Internet protocols. When and if this will actually happen is a hotly debated topic.
ISOC	The Internet Society: a membership organization whose members support a world-wide information network. It is also the governing body to which the IAB reports.
Leased line	See "dedicated line."
link	A connection between two points; a communications link.
mail reflector	A special mail address; electronic mail sent to this address is automatically forwarded to a set of other addresses. Typically, used to implement a mail discussion group.
MILNET	One of the DDN networks that make up the Internet; devoted to non-classified military (U.S.) communications. It was built using the same technology as the ARPAnet, and remained in production when the ARPAnet was decommissioned.
modem	A piece of equipment that connects a computer to a data transmission line (typically a telephone line of some sort). Normal people use modems that transfer data at speeds ranging from 1200 bits-per-second (bps) to 19.2 kbps. There are also modems providing higher speeds and supporting other media. These are used for special purposes—for example, to connect a large local network to its network provider over a leased line.
NIC	(a) Network Information Center; any organization that's responsible for supplying information about any network. (b) The InterNIC, which plays an important role in overall Internet coordination.

NOC

Network Operations Center; a group which is responsible for the day-to-day care and feeding of a network. Each service provider usually has a separate NOC, so you need to know which one to call when you have problems.

NREN

The National Research and Education Network; a U.S. effort to combine networks operated by different federal agencies into a single high-speed network. While this transition will be of significant technical and historical importance, it should have no effect on the typical Internet user.

NSFNET

The National Science Foundation Network; the NSFNET is *not* the Internet. It's just one of the networks that make up the Internet.

OSI

Open Systems Interconnect; another set of network protocols. See "ISO."

packet

A bundle of data. On the Internet, data is broken up into small chunks, called "packets"; each packet traverses the network independently. Packet sizes can vary from roughly 40 to 32000 bytes, depending on network hardware and media, but packets are normally less than 1500 bytes long.

POP

Point of Presence; the closest location for a network or telephone company (much like the local post office). Vendors will charge you based on how far you are from their local POP.

port

(a) A number that identifies a particular Internet application. When your computer sends a packet to another computer, that packet contains information about what protocol it's using (e.g., TCP or UDP), and what application it's trying to communicate with. The "port number" identifies the application. (b) One of a computer's physical input/output channels (i.e., a plug on the back). Unfortunately, these two meanings are completely unrelated. The first is more common when you're talking about the Internet (as in "*telnet* to port 1000"); the second is more common when you're talking about hardware ("connect your modem to the serial port on the back of your computer.")

posting
An individual article sent to a USENET (q.v.) news group; or the act of sending an article to a USENET news group.

PPP
Point-to-Point Protocol; a protocol that allows a computer to use the TCP/IP (Internet) protocols (and become a full-fledged Internet member) with a standard telephone line and a high-speed modem. PPP is a new standard for this which replaces SLIP (q.v.). Although PPP is less common than SLIP, it's quickly increasing in popularity.

protocol
A protocol is just a definition for how computers will act when talking to each other. Protocol definitions range from how bits are placed on a wire to the format of an electronic mail message. Standard protocols allow computers from different manufacturers to communicate; the computers can use completely different software, providing that the programs running on both ends agree on what the data means.

RFC
Request for Comments; a set of papers in which the Internet's standards, proposed standards and generally agreed-upon ideas are documented and published.

router
A system that transfers data between two networks that use the same protocols. The networks may differ in physical characteristics (e.g., a router may transfer data between an Ethernet and a leased telephone line).

server
(a) Software that allows a computer to offer a service to another computer. Other computers contact the server program by means of matching client (q.v.) software. (b) The computer on which the server software runs.

service provider	An organization that provides connections to a part of the Internet. If you want to connect your company's network, or even your personal computer, to the Internet, you have to talk to a "service provider."
shell	On a UNIX system, software that accepts and processes command lines from your terminal. UNIX has multiple shells available (e.g., C shell, Bourne shell, Korn shell), each with slightly different command formats and facilities.
signature	A file, typically five lines long or so, that people often insert at the end of electronic mail messages or USENET news articles. A signature contains, minimally, a name and an e-mail address. Signatures usually also contain postal addresses, and often contain silly quotes, pictures, and other things. Some are very elaborate, though signatures more than five or six lines long are in questionable taste.
SLIP	Serial Line IP; a protocol that allows a computer to use the Internet protocols (and become a full-fledged Internet member) with a standard telephone line and a high-speed modem. SLIP is being superseded by PPP (q.v.), but still in common use.
shell account	A type of interface on a dialup connection in which you login to the host computer and use a command shell to get to the Internet.
switched access	A network connection that can be created and destroyed as needed. Dialup connections are the simplest form of switched connections. SLIP or PPP also are commonly run over switched connections.
T1	1.544 mbps service (24 DS0s). Sometimes called "High-Cap," "T-Span," or "T-carrier."
T3	44.736 mbps service (28 T1s).
TCP	The Transmission Control Protocol. One of the protocols on which the Internet is based. For the technoids, TCP is a connection-oriented reliable protocol.
TCP/IP	The Transmission Control Protocol (see TCP), and the Internet Protocol (see IP).

TELNET	(a) A "terminal emulation" protocol that allows you to log in to other computer systems on the Internet. (b) An application program that allows you to log in to another computer system using the TELNET protocol. TELNET is described in detail in Chapter 5, *Remote Login.*
time out	A time out is what happens when two computers are "talking" and one computer—for any reason—fails to respond. The other computer will keep on trying for a certain amount of time, but will eventually "give up."
UNIX	A popular operating system that was very important in the development of the Internet. Contrary to rumor, though, you do *not* have to use UNIX to use the Internet. There are various flavors of UNIX. Two common ones are BSD and System V.
USENET	The USENET is an informal, rather anarchic, group of systems that exchange "news." News is essentially similar to "bulletin boards" on other networks. USENET actually predates the Internet, but these days, the Internet is used to transfer much of the USENET's traffic.
UUCP	UNIX-to-UNIX copy; a facility for copying files between UNIX systems, on which mail and USENET news services were built. While UUCP is still useful, the Internet provides a better way to do the same job.
WAIS	Wide-Area Information Servers; a very powerful system for looking up information in databases (or libraries) across the Internet.
White Pages	Lists of Internet users that are accessible through the Internet.
WWW	World-Wide Web; a hypertext-based system for finding and accessing Internet resources.

Bibliography

Introductory Materials

Books

Dern, Daniel. *The Internet Guide For New Users*, McGraw-Hill, 1993; ISBN: Trade paperback 007-016-511-4; hardcover 007-016-510-6.

Hahn, Harley. *A Student's Guide to Unix*, McGraw-Hill, Inc., 1993; ISBN 0-07-025511-3.

Hardie, Edward T. L. and Neou, Vivian, editors.*Internet: Mailing Lists*, 1993; ISBN 0-13-327941-3.

Kehoe, Brendan P. *Zen and the Art of the Internet: A Beginner's Guide*, Prentice-Hall, 1992; ISBN 0-13-010778-6.

Krol, Ed. *The Whole Internet User's Guide & Catalog*, O'Reilly & Associates, Inc., 1992; ISBN 1-56592-025-2.

LaQuey, Tracy and Ryer, Jeanne C. *The Internet Companion: A Beginner's Guide to Global Networking*, Addison-Wesley, 1992; ISBN 0-201-62224-6.

Marine, April, Kirkpatrick, Susan, Neou, Vivian and Ward, Carol, editors. *Internet: Getting Started*, Prentice Hall, 1993; ISBN 0-13-327933-2.

Tennant, Roy, Ober, John and Lipow, Anne G. Foreword by Lynch, Clifford.

Crossing the Internet Threshold: an Instructional Handbook, 1993; ISBN 1-882208-01-3.

Magazine

Internet World (1-800-MECKLER or meckler@jvnc.net for subscription info).

Online Materials

FYI RFC series. Contact InterNIC at 1-800-876-2373 or info@internic.net for retrieval information.

Global Network Navigator, O'Reilly & Associates. Send mail to gnn@ora.com.

Kehoe, Brendan P. *Zen and the Art of the Internet: A Beginner's Guide.* Contact InterNIC at 1-800-876-2373 or info@internic.net for retrieval information.

Technical Materials

Books

Albitz, Paul and Liu, Cricket. *DNS and BIND*, O'Reilly & Associates, Inc. 1993; ISBN 1-56592-010-4.

Comer, Douglas E. *Internetworking With TCP/IP, Volume I: Principles, Protocols, and Architecture*, Second Edition, Prentice Hall, 1991; ISBN 0-13-468505-9.

Garfinkel, Simson and Spafford, Gene. *Practical UNIX Security*, O'Reilly & Associates, Inc. 1991; IBSN 0-937175-72-2.

Hunt, Craig. *TCP/IP Network Administration*, O'Reilly & Associates, Inc., 1992; ISBN 0-937175-82-X.

Lynch, Daniel C. and Rose, Marshall T. *Internet System Handbook*, Addison-Wesley, 1993; IBSN 0-201-56741-5.

Online Materials

SLIP Setup Information for Dialup. FTP from boombox.micro.umn.edu, get pub/slip/phone.doc

FAQ on TCP/IP for PCs. FTP from netcom1.netcom.com, get pub/mail-com/IBMTCP/ibmtcp.zip

FAQ on TCP/IP packages for DOS and Windows Computers. FTP from ftp.cac.psu.edu, get pub/dos/info/tcpip.packages

Index of Macintosh Information. FTP from sumex-aim.stanford.edu, get info-mac/comm/Information/00info-abstracts.abs

Index

X

Y

Z

About the Author

Susan Estrada has been involved in the Internet since 1985 with over fifteen years in the telecommunications business. In 1988, she founded and built CERFnet, an Internet service provider located in San Diego, California. She was involved with the planning for the original NSFNET in 1985, when 56 kilobit per second links were considered to be high-speed and cost ten times more than they do today. Susan has been active in Internet organizations such as the Internet Society where she is currently a member of the Board of Trustees, FARNET, CIX, IESG, and IETF. She enjoys teaching various classes about the Internet, and currently is president of Aldea Communications, Inc.

Susan has a home in San Diego with her husband who has a different last name, two children, a dog, a fish, and a rabbit.

Colophon

Our look is the result of reader comments, our own experimentation, and feedback from distribution channels.

Distinctive covers complement our distinctive approach to technical topics, breathing personality and life into potentially dry subjects. UNIX and its attendant programs can be unruly beasts. Nutshell Handbooks help you tame them.

Edie Freedman designed the cover and the entire UNIX bestiary that appears on other Nutshell Handbooks. The images are adapted from 19th-century engravings from the Dover Pictorial Archive. The cover layout was produced with Quark XPress 3.1 using the ITC Garamond font.

The inside layout was formatted in FrameMaker 3.1 by Mike Sierra using ITC Garamond Light and ITC Garamond Book fonts. The figures were created in Aldus FreeHand 3.1 by Chris Reilley.

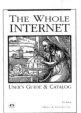

E-mail ordering is quick and easy. Simply fill out this application, and FAX or mail it to us at address or number below. We will notify you of your account number, which you will use whenever you order. When you place an order, an O'Reilly customer service representative will verify and acknowledge your order by e-mail. Questions? Comments? Call us at 800/998-9938 or e-mail us at order@ora.com

For ORA use only:

Account #

1) Shipping Address

Company Name (if applicable)

Name

Address

City/State/Zip

Country

Telephone (daytime)

FAX

2) Payment Information

❏ VISA   ❏ Mastercard   ❏ American Express

Credit Card Number

Expiration Date (very important)

Signature

2) Shipping Instructions

Specify your preferred method of shipping. Call or contact order@ora.com for shipping charges.

❏ UPS Standard   ❏ US Priority Mail

❏ Fed Ex Overnight   ❏ Int'l Air

❏ Fed Ex Economy   ❏ Book Rate

Special Instructions

4) User's name

Authorized User's Name

E-mail Address (legible, please)

O'Reilly & Associates, Inc.

103A Morris Street Sebastopol, California 95472
800/ 998-9938 • 707/829-0515 • FAX 707/829-0104 • order@ora.com

Books That Help People Get More Out of Computers

Please send me the following:

❏ A free catalog of titles.

❏ A list of Bookstores in my area that carry your books (U.S. and Canada only).

❏ A list of book distributors outside the U.S. and Canada.

❏ Information about consulting services for documentation or programming.

❏ Information about bundling books with my product.

❏ On-line descriptions of your books.

Name _____

Address _____

_____

City _____

State, ZIP _____

Country _____

Phone _____

Email Address_____
(Internet or Uunet)

Books That Help People Get More Out of Computers

Please send me the following:

❏ A free catalog of titles.

❏ A list of Bookstores in my area that carry your books (U.S. and Canada only).

❏ A list of book distributors outside the U.S. and Canada.

❏ Information about consulting services for documentation or programming.

❏ Information about bundling books with my product.

❏ On-line descriptions of your books.

Name _____

Address _____

_____

City _____

State, ZIP _____

Country _____

Phone _____

Email Address_____
(Internet or Uunet)

NAME_____

COMPANY_____

ADDRESS_____

CITY_____ STATE_____ ZIP_____

‖‖‖‖

BUSINESS REPLY MAIL

FIRST CLASS MAIL PERMIT NO. 80 SEBASTOPOL, CA

POSTAGE WILL BE PAID BY ADDRESSEE

O'REILLY & ASSOCIATES, INC.

103 Morris Street Suite A
Sebastopol CA 95472-9902

‖|‖‖|‖|‖|‖|‖‖‖|‖|‖|‖|‖|‖|‖|‖|‖‖|‖|‖|‖|‖‖‖|‖‖‖|‖|‖|‖|

NAME_____

COMPANY_____

ADDRESS_____

CITY_____ STATE_____ ZIP_____

‖‖‖‖

BUSINESS REPLY MAIL

FIRST CLASS MAIL PERMIT NO. 80 SEBASTOPOL, CA

POSTAGE WILL BE PAID BY ADDRESSEE

O'REILLY & ASSOCIATES, INC.

103 Morris Street Suite A
Sebastopol CA 95472-9902

‖|‖‖|‖|‖|‖|‖|‖‖‖|‖|‖|‖|‖|‖|‖|‖|‖‖|‖|‖|‖|‖‖‖|‖‖‖|‖|‖|‖|